I Choose You Today

31 Choices to Make Love Last

Deb DeArmond

Abingdon Press

Nashville

I CHOOSE YOU TODAY
31 Choices to Make Love Last

No part of this work may be reproduced or transmitted in any form or by any means, electronic or mechanical, including photocopying and recording, or by any information storage or retrieval system, except as may be expressly permitted by the 1976 Copyright Act or in writing from the publisher. Requests for permission can be addressed to Permissions, The United Methodist Publishing House, P.O. Box 801, 201 Eighth Avenue South, Nashville, TN 37202-0801, or e-mailed to permissions@umpublishing.org.

Throughout this book, releases have been secured whenever real names have been used, but in all other instances, names and identifying details have been changed—and sometimes composites were created—to protect the privacy of the actual individuals. While the story of the couple in chapter 7 is real, their names are fictitious, as the author was drawing from memory regarding a television documentary seen approximately fifteen years ago. Every attempt has been made to locate the source, but without success. If you have any information, please contact the publisher so that further details can be included in future printings.

Library of Congress Cataloging-in-Publication Data

ISBN 978-1-4267-8796-6

Unless otherwise noted, scripture quotations are taken from the Common English Bible. Copyright © 2011 by the Common English Bible. All rights reserved. Used by permission. www.CommonEnglishBible.com.

Scripture quotations marked NLT are taken from the Holy Bible, New Living Translation, copyright © 1996, 2004, 2007. Used by permission of Tyndale House Publishers, Inc., Carol Stream, Illinois 60188. All rights reserved.

Scripture quotations from THE MESSAGE. Copyright © by Eugene H. Peterson 1993, 1994, 1995, 1996, 2000, 2001, 2002. Used by permission of NavPress Publishing Group.

Scripture quotations marked "NKJV™" are taken from the New King James Version®. Copyright © 1982 by Thomas Nelson, Inc. Used by permission. All rights reserved.

Scripture quotation marked AMP taken from the Amplified® Bible, Copyright © 1954, 1958, 1962, 1964, 1965, 1987 by The Lockman Foundation. Used by permission. (www.Lockman.org)

Scripture quotations marked (NIV) are from the Holy Bible, New International Version®, NIV® Copyright © 1973, 1978, 1984, 2011 by Biblica, Inc.® Used by permission. All rights reserved worldwide.

Scripture quotations marked (ESV) are from The Holy Bible, English Standard Version® (ESV®), copyright © 2001 by Crossway, a publishing ministry of Good News Publishers. Used by permission. All rights reserved.

15 16 17 18 19 20 21 22 23 24—10 9 8 7 6 5 4 3 2 1
MANUFACTURED IN THE UNITED STATES OF AMERICA

CONTENTS

For Jesus, because he chose me.

IT'S A MATTER OF CHOICE

There are times in life you make a commitment to something without fully understanding what that entails. Kind of a leap of faith, a *let's roll with the punches and hope for the best* sort of deal. I've been there, and I'll bet you have too.

We recently returned from our annual family vacation. I mean the w-h-o-l-e family. Three adult sons, their wives (one of whom is pregnant), and two young grandsons. It involved a three-hour flight, one rented vacation house, two rental cars, and a huge amount of luggage. We did the beach and Disney and Universal Studios; some saw a *Tonight Show* taping while others headed to a concert in San Diego. We knew going into the week there might be some moments when we became frustrated or impatient with one another. As a family, we can be a bit dramatic, so we weren't blindsided when it happened.

But it was at sundown on the sands of Corona Del Mar that things took an unexpected turn...

We engaged a talented young photographer to snap some family photos on the beach just as the sun was setting. Each son, his wife, and baby (one still hitching a ride in Mama's tummy) took a place in front of the lens to capture a special moment at the edge of the Pacific.

At last, my hubby and I stepped up to have our picture taken. The photographer positioned us, asked us to kiss, and then something odd happened...my husband took a knee. Literally, he fell to his knees in front of me. For a brief moment I thought to myself, *Oh, Lord! He's having a stroke!* But I quickly realized my concern was misplaced when I saw him produce a beautiful ring box from his pocket.

"Would you do it all again with me?" he asked. "Would you still choose to marry me?"

I was stunned. The kids all stood nearby, whistling and clapping. Apparently, they had been in on the surprise. I was completely caught off guard, but I negotiated the lump in my throat and finally found my voice. "Yes, sweetheart. I'd do it again. I still choose you."

He beamed. I cried a little. Then I reached for the ring.

He did good. Clearly, he had been taking notes as I browsed jewelry-store windows at the mall. It's one of the things I love about this man: he has a giving heart. We finished the evening with a fabulous dinner on the beach in Laguna—one of my favorite places on the planet—surrounded by the 8.5 people most important to us.

But the best part of the night for me came later, as we sat and talked about our evening.

"What on earth gave you the idea to do this?" I asked him. "You never even proposed thirty-eight years ago." We met young and just knew we were supposed to marry, so we simply began making wedding plans.

"I know," he said with a grin. "You didn't have a proposal story. Every woman should have a proposal story, and I wanted you to have one. This is yours, even if it's a little late."

Somehow, that made it even better.

At nineteen, when we got engaged, we didn't know *anything*. I mean it when I say *we knew nothing* about what life would bring our way. We had no clue that marriage would be a full-time job requiring energy and effort we didn't know we could produce, much less sustain.

We hadn't envisioned babies with ear infections at two in the morning or caring for elderly parents while raising our children. Layoffs, second mortgages, braces, and college tuition. Moments that pushed us hard and occasionally created conflict between us. It wasn't always easy, but it was always worth the effort—made possible because we did it *together*.

So when the question came, "Would you do it all again?" it was with a full understanding of what those thirty-seven-plus years of life together meant. That my husband would desire to repeat it all meant the world to me. The fact I was still able to say yes without hesitation tells our story. We love one another fiercely.

Love is not a feeling, and neither is marriage. Each is a choice—one that must be made every single day, even if it's spoken through gritted teeth. And we are smart enough to know we could never manage on our own; we are very clear: united in Christ is how we started and how we will have to continue if we plan to finish strong. And that *is* our plan.

> It's an act of our will to choose our marriage, day in and day out.

It's an act of our will to choose our marriage, day in and day out. And it is God's grace that makes that choice possible. Those couples whose marriages thrive have learned the secret: it's all in the choices you make.

And sweetheart, I choose you, again today.

****

What's the secret for hanging on to the *happily ever after* feelings from the day you said, "I do"? It could be as simple as four little words: "I choose you today."

Proverbs 18:21 reminds us that "death and life are in the power of the tongue." Words have the power to create. God *spoke* the world and life itself into existence. We enter into life in Christ by a *confession* of our mouth. Faith spoken moves mountains. Our words can bless or curse. *Words count.*

What if we chose to bless—not curse—our union, regardless of our feelings in the moment?

James tells us: "A word out of your mouth may seem of no account, but it can accomplish nearly anything—or destroy it!" (James 3:5 *THE MESSAGE*).

What will you choose today?

This book is based on a simple principle that marriage is always a *choice*—one that benefits from a daily renewal of our commitment to one another. Christ followers are charged to live in God's truth. Feelings are not the foundation for truth; feelings are subject to change. God's Word is the foundation for truth.

The title of this book is based on the traditional line included in the wedding ceremony: *"I choose you to be my lawfully wedded husband [or wife], to have and to hold . . ."* Choice is a gift from God. God expects us to *choose* marriage, *choose* our spouse, and *choose* to live in a way that is pleasing to him. It is then, and only then, we will live the life God meant for us to enjoy.

The book was designed for use in multiple ways.

- As a married couple, read the text and scripture together and discuss the answers to the action-planning questions. You may elect to read it and complete the questions separately and then come together to discuss the chapter.
- As an engaged couple, use this book as you prepare for marriage. Many couples spend more time planning the wedding than readying themselves for what is likely to be the biggest change they will ever experience in life, short of conversion to life in Christ. Work through the chapters and discuss your experiences as a couple as well as the family models you grew up with.
- You may desire a deeper, more meaningful relationship with your spouse but are the only one committed to exploring those possibilities through a devotional process. Even if you are working through the chapters and activities alone, you will find tremendous benefit for your marriage.
- The book works well for a small group or Bible study. A leader's guide can be found on the author's website at http://www.debdearmond.com.

I encourage you to read through the table of contents and choose the topics that would provide the greatest benefit to your marriage at this time or are of the highest interest to you. Don't rush through the chapters; rather, allow yourself time to fulfill the commitments you've made at the end of one chapter before moving on to the next. Doing so will provide encouragement and momentum in exercising your God-given gift of choice. I'd suggest you focus on no more than one topic a week.

You've already begun to choose wisely—you've chosen to examine how your words can impact your marriage and your life. Remember, it could be as simple as four little words...

I choose you today.

> *Conventional wisdom: "Happily ever after is not a fairy tale. It's a choice."*
> —FAWN WEAVER

I CHOOSE TO ACCEPT GOD'S WORD AS THE BLUEPRINT FOR OUR LIFE

Every scripture is inspired by God and is useful for teaching, for showing mistakes, for correcting, and for training character.
—2 TIMOTHY 3:16

"But do you *really* think God is going to be mad at us if we go to this movie?" Jacqui was frustrated that, once again, Brian had pulled the faith card. It was happening often these days. "Everyone from work has seen it—I even heard some people from church say it was really good. I'd like to see it too. Come on, Brian! What can it really hurt?"

"I'm just not personally comfortable with it," he responded. "The rating is based on sexual content, violence, and I've heard the language is bad—really bad. It's used throughout the movie, not just in one or two spots." Brian's expression let Jacqui know he wasn't about to change his mind.

She reluctantly and loudly withdrew, making certain he could hear her murmuring as she slammed the door to their bedroom. The weekend was getting off to a bad start.

Brian was tired of being the enforcer, or as Jacqui called him, *the spoiler*. Yet their conflicts were occurring more often. The tension had started a few months after their relocation for Brian's promotion. They fought about their giving, their lifestyle—things that had never been an issue before—and Brian was concerned. *Why are we constantly arguing? And what will it take for us to get on the same page?*

Life for the couple had become increasingly difficult following the move from their hometown. Living away from the community and the church where they had grown up had been a big adjustment—it had taken longer than expected to find a new church they could agree on.

Even after the decision was made, Jacqui questioned whether it was the right fit for them. Brian too had to admit things were different at this church—the worship was a little over the top and the people came dressed very casually. *Different isn't wrong; it's just not what you're used to,* he often reminded himself. Still, it didn't feel like home yet.

Attending the same church with both of their extended families over the years had created a set of unspoken expectations. The couple had never stopped to ask, "Are we going to church this weekend?" It was a given. "Will we participate in the annual missions outreach or sing in the choir?" had not been discussed. He and Jacqui had simply followed the pattern established by their families.

They had been good patterns, but Brian became increasingly aware that church in their hometown had been a comfortable routine, a family tradition, almost a social network. Rather than making a daily commitment born of their mutual desire to grow in Christ and walk as Jesus walked, he and Jacqui had continued their family patterns once married. Now the couple was on their own for the first time, not just geographically but spiritually. There were conversations they'd never had, issues they had not discussed; and at this point, it showed.

Ultimately Brian realized his discomfort had little to do with their new town or the new church. He began to see that he and Jacqui had done more than move geo-

> ❧
>
> *God's blueprint for successful marriage is readily available. It's called the Bible.*

graphically. Their hearts had moved as well—away from many of the godly principles they had been taught as kids and relied on all their lives. Now the two of them were wrestling with that reality.

"God's Word is the user's manual for life," their former youth pastor always said. *Well then, the manual's a little dusty.* Brian knew that everything he and Jacqui needed to sort it all out was available to them if they would search their Bibles and seek God in prayer.

God had been tugging on Jacqui's heart as well. She approached Brian later that evening. "I'm not sure where to start, Brian, but we've got to find our way back to us."

Brian agreed. "I'm so sorry, babe. I didn't realize we had gotten so off track. I guess it's time we grow up and get clear about God's plan for us as a couple. I'm willing to figure out what that should look like, aren't you?"

"You and I won't always agree on everything," Jacqui said softly, "but if we choose to agree that God will have the final word in our household, I can live with that." She slipped her hand into his. "There's a new small group for young marrieds starting next week. Interested?"

Conventional wisdom: "When everything else fails, read the instructions."

—UNKNOWN

Chapter 1 Choice Questions:
I Choose to Accept God's Word as the Blueprint for Our Life

1. Do a quick inventory: Are you and your spouse living in a way that honors God and his Word as the blueprint in your life? List the reasons for your response.
2. What practices or lifestyle choices have created conflict or have been difficult to deal with at times? How have you dealt with them in the past?
3. What will you need to do to accept God's Word as the final authority over opinions, popular thought, or outside pressure?

Use the prayer below to declare your choice—or create one of your own.

Prayer: Father, you gave us your Word to provide direction, insight, and understanding on how to live and walk in this life. The Bible is not a list of don't dos designed to keep us from having fun. It's a book of life, filled with hope and promise for those who choose it. I am committed to following your example in all things, resisting customs, traditions, and popular opinion. I will honor you by following the user's manual you lovingly created, knowing this brings great reward and joy. I choose today to accept your Word and submit to it as the authority in my life.

CHAPTER 2

I CHOOSE TO PURSUE YOU

As for husbands, love your wives just like Christ loved the church and gave himself for her.

—EPHESIANS 5:25

Another business trip, another city. The worst part of that first day on the road is taking my clothes out of the suitcase, hanging them up, and pressing those that didn't fare well during travel. I had just mentioned to my husband, Ron, that morning how much I dreaded that sometimes-twice-a-week task as I moved between client locations.

Now, as I pulled the *advertised* no-wrinkle blouse from my bag, an envelope fluttered to the floor. I fetched it from the carpet as I threw the blouse in the ironing pile.

Ron's handwriting: *Mag.* His pet name made me smile immediately. I sank down on the foot of the bed and turned the envelope over. "I love you" was written across the sealed flap.

A sweet note inside reminded me of his love for me, how much he missed me every second I was gone and how he dreaded the empty side of the bed. A little flirting, a little prayer for my upcoming week. A sweet surprise, but not the first. Ron has pursued me consistently in the past thirty-eight years.

He's the romantic; I'm pragmatic. He can recall the date of our first kiss and never forgets an anniversary or special occasion. He has created elaborate romantic surprises for me over the years, capturing my heart again and again.

I could take a page from his book. I've been guilty sometimes of saying to him the morning of his birthday, "I didn't get you a card. Will a kiss do?"

I should be better at this. I grew up in a home where every day my father said to my mom, "Dottie, did I tell you today I love you?" She always responded: "Yes, but you can tell me again." They were perfect together. Mom often appeared annoyed when Dad (in his seventies) would say to the waiter, "Hey there, buddy, look around. The most beautiful girl in the room is with me tonight." She said it embarrassed her, but truthfully, she loved every romantic moment.

You are hard to resist when you're chasing your spouse's heart.

Ron's envelope got me to thinking about the impact his pursuit has made on me. Knowing he always has me at the forefront of his thoughts and affections has created a great confidence, not only in our relationship but also for me personally. I'm not twenty-five anymore, but he still sees me as beautiful; he is still attracted to me. I trust his heart, if not always his eyes!

I'm so glad it's his heart he uses when he looks at me. I never wonder whether or not he truly loves me, needs me, and wants me. His pursuit speaks volumes, and it draws me to him time after time.

Doesn't he deserve the same from me? That confidence that comes from being relentlessly pursued? He owns my heart; he knows it. But I want him to *feel* it. I want him to experience the same confidence and assurance his pursuit affords me. I want him to know that my affection and attraction to him have not only remained steady, but they've grown over the years.

I know Ephesians 5:25—with its directive to give up ourselves just as Christ did for the church—is addressed to husbands, but Romans 8:29 says, "For God knew his people in advance, and he chose them to become like his Son" (NLT). God is in relentless pursuit of those he loves. God sent Jesus to pursue us and I am *called to follow his lead*—to pursue those I love.

So what does it mean to engage in a pursuit? The dictionary defines pursue as: *to follow and try to catch or capture (someone or something) for usually a long distance or time*. I want to capture my someone's heart for a *very* long time. I want to be in love with Ron every day I draw breath.

I will admit, it doesn't come naturally for me. I'm a list maker, a busy girl, and I'm not necessarily wired for pursuit. So it's a choice I want to make on a regular basis—even if I have to plan it. Spontaneity is overrated anyway.

I find Ron hard to resist when he's chasing my heart. I'm betting I can create a major distraction when *I'm* in full pursuit.

So…what will you choose?

> *Conventional wisdom: "She chased and chased me until I caught her."*
>
> —LARRY GRAEME (MY DAD!)

Chapter 2 Choice Questions: I Choose to Pursue You

1. Does pursuing your spouse come naturally for you? Does he/she pursue you? Record your thoughts about how willingly and consistently you pursue your spouse.
2. What's standing in the way of intentional pursuit (time, personality, issues, hurts/disappointments)? Are you willing to set this aside? What needs to be addressed in prayer or forgiveness?
3. Have a conversation with your spouse, asking the following questions:
   - Do you feel pursued? What makes you feel the way you do?
   - How confident are you about my affection for you? My attraction to you? My commitment to you and our marriage?
   - What is the best way to communicate my attraction and commitment?

Use the prayer below to declare your choice—or create one of your own.

Prayer: Father, thank you for pursuing me. I choose to follow your example and pursue the one I love. I want to know I am valued and desired in my marriage, and I want that same confidence for my husband/wife. I accept that love is not a feeling; it's an action, a choice each day. Help me through your Spirit to make that choice. I ask you to encourage me in my role as pursuer. I will set aside the busyness of home, kids, and work to communicate affection and attraction for my spouse. And even if it's not my own personal style, it's your style—one I ask you to mature in me.

CHAPTER 3

I CHOOSE TO LOVE YOU

Rushing waters can't quench love; rivers can't wash it away. If someone gave all his estate in exchange for love, he would be laughed to utter shame.

—Song of Songs 8:7

Sam slammed the door with gusto, making sure it was loud enough for Bethany to hear. *She's not reasonable, and when she gets upset, she just freezes me out. I'm tired of it. Actually, I'm tired of her. Where's the cute redhead I fell in love with?*

He wasn't quite sure where their lives were headed, but he couldn't live this way any longer. He hated the silent treatment, especially when he was trying to help Bethany understand the situation. His demanding job put him under the microscope. There had been client complaints about his work, and with their efforts to start a family, the last thing they needed was to lose his job and their insurance.

I don't love her anymore? What a joke! Can't she see that I'm doing this for us? For her?

In the now-quiet house, Bethany sat on the side of the bed, startled by the explosive slam of the front door. Her thoughts turned quickly to last night's conversation. It ended with Sam pleading his case, but she'd heard enough. Despite his attempts to continue the conversation—she turned away, refusing to talk. Then sleep eluded her as she replayed it over and over in her head.

The next morning, when he asked about her plans for the day, she remained silent. It was Saturday, and he was heading to the office—again. *He doesn't want to spend time with me. He's using work as an excuse. All he does is work, eat, sleep, and make excuses for why he's too tired for any time together.*

He's certainly not the same guy I married. What happened to Mr. Romance? When was the last time he surprised me with flowers? It doesn't feel like Sam loves me anymore. Not like he used to. If I'm really honest, I'm not sure I feel the same way about him either. Could be we've run our course. Perhaps it's a good thing the fertility treatments have failed—maybe it's God's way of telling us we're done.

Life is pressing on Bethany and Sam, and she's entertaining a lie. God doesn't throw in the towel on love.

When Mr. Romance and the cute redhead fell in love, life was easy. Back then, they were silly and affectionate, once caught kissing behind the Christmas tree. Friends and family jokingly warned them, "The honeymoon won't last forever." But Sam and Bethany ignored the warnings. Their relationship was God-centered and their marriage commitment was based on the Lord's presence in their lives. This was a love that would last a lifetime.

So what happened? Life happened.

The shock of infertility and the stress to conceive gradually replaced the sweet warmth of their relationship. Intimacy is now determined by the calendar rather than their desire for closeness and connection. They feel cornered by their circumstances and are desperate to experience something other than disappointment and the fear that pregnancy will never happen. And they are desperate to sense the love they once shared.

Spend your time listening deeply, noticing, and bringing out the best in the person sitting across from you. This is where the love magic happens.

It's an incredible feeling to be loved without constraint and to return that love without reservation. But love itself is not a feeling—feelings are subject to change. Financial problems, illness, aging parents who need help, or issues like those experienced by Bethany and Sam create strong feelings that can force their way to the forefront. The focus on actively loving one another slips aside as we deal with the issues that threaten to consume us. Instead of clinging together during difficulty, couples often spiral apart. We no longer feel loved; we no longer feel like loving. Let that continue long enough and the marriage is at risk.

Love is an act of our will, based on the commitment we made when we married. But that commitment is not a *one-and-done* kind of deal. It must be renewed. Daily. Love is a choice. Give it or give up on it. Love is *always* a choice.

When we choose to love one another, honoring our commitment in obedience to God, a startling transformation takes place. The ability to be open, kind, and loving (or the willingness, if the "want to" isn't quite there) is once again possible. When we align our hearts with God's plan and purpose, he surprises us and rekindles the connection we crave. We *feel* it once again. And we *do* want to feel it.

My friends Becky and Greg Johnson know a little something about love. They found it later in life, each having a previous marriage that did not survive. So this second chance to experience what Greg calls "mad, stupid love" is a rich gift indeed. Becky recently shared their secret with me:

> Do you know why we really fall in love with someone? And do you know what *keeps* people in love for a lifetime? It has very little to do with your looks, charm, or talent. As an almost-old woman, I will tell you the truth. I know the secret weapon to falling in love and staying there: people fall in love because of the way the other person makes them feel about *themselves*. Someone who makes you feel smart, beautiful, talented, and kind (whether or not you really *are* any of these things) when you are together is pretty much irresistible. Don't waste time trying to impress someone. Spend your time listening deeply, noticing, and bringing out the best in the person sitting across from you. When two people both do this for each other every day, well, this is where the love magic happens.

The *love magic*.

There will be days—oh, yes, there will—when you might not feel loved and don't feel like loving. It happens. Change the pattern by changing your mind and your conversation. Make the commitment to love, and start by saying, "I choose you today."

Conventional wisdom: "So it's not gonna be easy. It's gonna be really hard. We're gonna have to work at this every day, but I want to do that because I want you. I want all of you, forever, you and me, every day."

—NICHOLAS SPARKS, THE NOTEBOOK

Chapter 3 Choice Questions: I Choose to Love You

1. Loving your spouse is an everyday commitment. How well are you renewing it daily?
2. What issues threaten to turn you away from your spouse? What steps can you take to turn toward one another during difficulties (praying together, having a weekly date, and so forth)?
3. How can you demonstrate your love for your spouse? What would be meaningful?

Use the prayer below to declare your choice—or create one of your own.

Prayer: Father, your love is perfect. It is sacrificial and never fails. You chose to love me even though I was undeserving, and you continue to love me even when I am unlovable. I commit today to follow your example with my spouse, knowing there may be times when it is a difficult choice. I will choose love as an act of my will.

CHAPTER 4

I CHOOSE TO BLESS YOU

Then he blessed the children and went away from there.
—MATTHEW 19:15

Cliff never left the house in the morning without saying good-bye," Trisha explained. "A quick kiss and a 'have a great day' on his way out the door. At 5:15 A.M., sometimes I slept right through it.

"But one morning, I heard something beyond the standard good-bye as he knelt at my side of the bed and spoke these words over me: 'Trisha, I love you very much. You are God's gift to me. May he bless you today in everything you do. May you be a blessing to others. Love ya.'"

Cliff's voice was soft, but she heard it—and it got her attention. I'm a gift? A gift to my husband from God? "Hearing that affirmation from my husband was a beautiful way to start my day."

The morning blessing continued the next day and the next. Cliff even began to bless Trisha when they sat down for meals, at home and in public. "He takes hold of my hands from across the table, looks into my eyes, and blesses our food and me, with words like, 'I'm blessed to have my beautiful wife with me to share this food. May God bless it for the nourishment of our bodies, and our bodies to his service. In Jesus' name. Amen.' I feel so valued when he does it."

So where did all of this come from?

Cliff and Trisha aren't newlyweds; they celebrated forty-one years of marriage last year. They married young without knowing one another well. He was a handsome Marine who pursued Trisha from the moment they met, proposing three weeks from that day. She was raised in church, but he was not. "I seemed to be the more spiritual one in the marriage, even though Cliff was a Christian," she says. "When times got tough, his walk of faith was weak."

Like most marriages, there were good times and bad, but they hung in, always active in church and working to keep God central in their relationship. Six years ago, Cliff became a serious student of the Word of God, and things began to change—for him and Trisha. Following the principles found in Ephesians 5:25, Cliff began to see his wife as his beloved, just as Christ sees the church, whom he calls his bride. "The bride of Christ is loved and honored and is called by his name—Christian," Trisha explains. "It's an honor to be identified as Cliff's bride; I am blessed to have taken on his name and be known as Mrs. Hare."

Bless, blessed, and blessing. These are familiar words, ones we use often. But what is a blessing? How is it defined and what does it mean? The Online Free Dictionary provides us these definitions:

- the act or words of a person who blesses.
- a special favor, mercy, or benefit: the blessings of liberty.
- a favor or gift bestowed by God, thereby bringing happiness.

- the invoking of God's favor upon a person.
- praise; devotion; worship, especially grace said before a meal.
- approval or good wishes.

God blessed Adam and Eve and said, "Be fertile and multiply." That was an expression of his favor—a benefit of their union, intended to bring them happiness. Even those not of faith are heard to say, "Bless you," when someone sneezes. It's a well-intentioned wish for health.

How do you begin blessing your spouse? Start with a simple declaration—a request for God's favor or an affirmation of the important role he or she plays in your life. Look at Cliff's words: "I'm blessed to have my beautiful wife. You are God's gift to me. May God bless you in everything you do. May you be a blessing to others."

Would you like to deepen your connection? Begin today with a decision and a few simple words: I choose to bless you today.

The words don't have to be fancy or poetic. Think sincere, positive, and offered to acknowledge and affirm. The blessing may be a statement of fact: "I thank you, Lord, that my wife is an outstanding mother and keeper of our home, blessing my life and that of our children." Or it could be a statement of faith, asking God's favor in your spouse's life, as in, "Heavenly Father, I thank you that my husband is a diligent provider. I ask that he is blessed today on his job and acknowledged for his faithfulness."

The positive impact of speaking the blessing aloud is hugely beneficial, as we see with Cliff and Trisha. "I am assured of my husband's love," she explains. "I have a sense of value and worth, that I am a gift packaged by God for my husband." What's more, *both* are blessed as a result. "We have a deeper love and respect for one another, and our home is more peaceful," Trisha says.

It's so easy to spot the flaws in others, to identify what we don't like in their behavior. Address those things in prayer and use a blessing to build up your husband or wife, providing support as they grow.

I saw a quote recently that said something quite profound: "You get more of what you affirm." When we affirm others, it encourages them to live up to the status we've praised. That's proven true for Cliff and Trisha. "Now my effort each day is to be that special gift to my husband," Trisha says. "Now I pray for God to show me what I can do to affirm Cliff, to let him know how much I love and respect him."

Would you welcome more love and respect in the relationship? Would you like to deepen the connection you share? It can begin today with a decision and a few simple words: *I choose to bless you today.*

> *Conventional wisdom: "Sometimes we focus so much on what we don't have that we fail to see, appreciate, and use what we do have!"*
>
> —JEFF DIXON

Chapter 4 Choice Questions:
I Choose to Bless You

1. What qualities, behaviors, and godly characteristics can you affirm in your husband or wife? What about him/her blesses you?
2. What favor can you ask God to bestow on your spouse? What attributes or actions would be beneficial for your spouse at this time in his/her life?
3. What steps will you take to begin blessing your spouse?

Use the prayer below to declare your choice—or create one of your own.

Prayer: Lord, thank you for blessing me with the husband/wife you've given me. My desire is to bless my spouse daily, holding his/her life before you so encouragement and boldness in you are the result. I choose to be a person who blesses, not curses, and I call favor into my husband's/wife's life. I will choose words that uplift, affirm, and acknowledge. I will declare what you've called into the life of my loved one, standing in faith that you are faithful to complete the good work you've begun. When I am tempted to be critical, I ask your Spirit to remind me of the truth in your Word and to bring a blessing to my lips instead.

CHAPTER 5

I CHOOSE TO HONOR YOU

Love each other like the members of your family. Be the best at showing honor to each other.
—ROMANS 12:10

W ell! Hello, Rosie! How is the *talented artist* today?" Jeff smiled at her startled expression and winked at her husband, Danny, across the room.

Rosie set her packages on the dining room table. "Hi, Jeff. If you're speaking to me," she laughed, "I'm just fine, thank you. How about you?"

"Better, now that I have the honor of spending time with such a *talented artist*." Again, the emphasis on the two words. Jeff glanced in Danny's direction and they began to laugh.

Rosie looked at her husband with raised eyebrows. "Okay, so what's the joke? I feel like I came in just a moment after the punch line, and somehow I think the joke's on me."

Danny quickly broke in, "No, babe. That's not it at all."

"I'm sorry, Rosie," Jeff added. "Ever since your show, Danny's been bragging on you nonstop. I'm not sure who's more excited about the success of your gallery showing—you or him." Jeff paused and punched his friend in the arm. "In truth, Rosie, it's been cool to hear Danny talk about it. He carries the art critic's review from the *Herald Tribune* in his pocket. It's the one that named you 'this year's most talented new artist.' He's kind of adopted that phrase when he talks about you. And boy, does he talk a *lot* about you! We're all so proud of you. Major congrats."

Rosie was stunned. Danny had always been supportive of her art, but he's a bit on the quiet side, so this came as a sweet surprise. His opinion of her work was more important to her than almost anyone's. Knowing he'd been speaking so positively about her made her feel…honored, far beyond any favorable review from an art critic.

Honor is defined as to regard with great respect; to acknowledge or commend in public or in private. Words like *compliment, credit, thank, praise, acclaim, applaud, cheer, salute, celebrate,* and *congratulate* are all used to describe this. In Rosie's case, her husband honored her for something she *accomplished*—her successful gallery showing. He also acknowledged her for who she *is*—an artist who uses her gift to honor the Lord.

> When we honor one another, we create an environment in our marriage that breeds trust, patience, and intimacy.

It's an important distinction, because honor is due in both cases.

Accomplishment is usually enjoyed as a result of effort and hard work, faithfully staying the course when things are difficult. When we honor our spouse's achievement, we reinforce the path he or she took and celebrate the successful outcome. Danny knew that at times Rosie was tempted to give up and walk away. Recognizing her commitment and determination in this situation helped build her confidence for the next opportunity.

Honoring *who they are* is important as well. Rosie's efforts may have been heroic—long nights dedicated to her art, years of time and money invested in developing her craft—but they did not guarantee the critic's acclaim. God has gifted Rosie and she has dedicated her art to the Lord. The gallery auction was a fundraiser for her church's battered women's shelter. Although the notoriety and success was fun, her heart's desire was always to create art that honors God and helps point people to the Savior.

Honor is an interesting concept. We may honor the president without ever meeting him. The honor is not based on a personal relationship; it's based on respect for the office he fills. God calls us to an even higher standard in marriage.

There is no other relationship on earth where we are so intimately on display. The mystery that existed in courtship disappears after a few years of marriage. A spouse *knows* who we are, warts and all—our pluses and minuses, weird habits, and shortcomings. Ever hear the phrase "Familiarity breeds contempt"? Sometimes what we know makes honor a tough go. It may be easier to honor those we don't know or don't know well. We know their *public face*—the one they share with the world.

Think about this example. If a guest in my home unknowingly tracks in mud as he enters and then apologizes, my reaction is to reassure him: "It's not a problem; it will vacuum right up when it's dry. Don't give it another thought." But if my husband muddied my carpets, my response might not be so pleasant: "What on earth were you thinking? Look at the mess you've made!" I've offered honor to a visitor, but not to the one who shares my home.

I'm grateful that the Savior, who knows me well—down to my innermost thoughts—does not take that approach. He knows me completely yet honors me with his love, his patience, and his presence in my life.

Honor is a choice. When we honor one another, we create an environment in our home and marriage that breeds trust, patience, and even intimacy. So as tempting as it may be to create a list to hand to your spouse on ways you'd like to be honored, how about if you go first? Here are a few ideas to get you started. (The *him/her and he/she* is not specific; they are interchangeable.)

1. Let him know he's important to you, identifying the traits that bless you most.
2. Focus on what she's doing right, not on the negatives.
3. Compliment him often. Be specific and go beyond flattery.
4. Acknowledge her efforts early in the process; don't wait for successful performance.
5. Express your appreciation for your spouse's work to help support the family.
6. Tell him how proud you are of the husband, father, or friend he is.
7. Brag about her to others, both in front of her and when she's not present.
8. Address issues privately, in a respectful tone.
9. Thank her for the way she cares for the kids or your home or how hard she works on the job. Thank him for cooking the great weekend breakfasts and for things he does around the house.

10. When things go wrong, don't say, "I told you so." Work instead to help find a solution.
11. Don't criticize one another in public. Keep each other's dignity intact.
12. Thank her for just being herself.

Remember, the Lord values your spouse, who was made in his image (Genesis 1:27). God *treasures* your mate (Exodus 19:5 NIV). It's wise to agree with God in this matter.

Honoring a spouse whose choices are not always honorable can be a challenge. Identify the traits and behaviors you can affirm, and do so. Pray about those issues you cannot praise and trust God to lead you. Let the Lord work on your spouse. Choose honor, and let God handle the results.

What will you choose today?

> *Conventional wisdom: "There has never been a statue erected to honor a critic."*
> —Zig Ziglar

Chapter 5 Choice Questions:
I Choose to Honor You

1. How well and how often do you honor your spouse? What prompts you to do it? Why do you sometimes fail to offer honor?
2. Examine the list of potential ways mentioned in the reading to honor your spouse. Place a ✓ next to those you do consistently well. Place an X next to those you don't do at all or could do more often.
3. What's your plan? What will you choose to do, starting today, to honor your mate?

Use the prayer below to declare your choice—or create one of your own.

Prayer: Thank you, Father, for blessing me with your love, your grace, and your mercy. I choose to acknowledge you as the Lord of my life. Because the Bible instructs us to honor one another, above even ourselves, I will choose to actively do so with my spouse. I desire to build an environment that creates intimacy and trust in our marriage, and I believe it cannot be accomplished without this important element of respect in the relationship. I ask you to reveal any behavior that is dishonoring, and I request your help to overcome it. Direct me to consistently choose words and actions that express honor to my spouse, even if it is not returned. I am willing to trust you for the results.

CHAPTER 6

I CHOOSE TO KEEP MY COMMITMENT TO YOU

When a man makes a solemn promise to the LORD or swears
a solemn pledge of binding obligation for himself, he cannot
break his word. He must do everything he said.

—NUMBERS 30:2

The December day was rainy and dark, but the room was flooded with candlelight. Our son, Jordan, was marrying his sweet Sarah. They had grown up together since age thirteen, and now they were standing at the altar, ready to make the commitment to spend their lives together. It was an unforgettable honor for my husband, Ron, to take part in the ceremony.

"Sarah, there are four things God asks of a believing wife. They are found in the fifth chapter of Ephesians." Ron looked into her eyes through the veil covering her face as he read them aloud. He smiled at her warmly. We had long loved Sarah and welcomed her fully into the family.

He turned to the groom, our son Jordan. "And son, God lays out his expectations of you as well. There are eight things..." His voice began to trail off. "And if I could see my notes to read them, I would." Ron removed his glasses and wiped the tears from his face with the back of his tuxedoed arm. Two hundred people collectively sighed. Ron cleared his throat and went on to describe the commitment God asks of a Christ-following husband.

"Why is the pastor crying?" Sarah's eighty-year-old grandmother whispered loudly.

True commitment, which is an active, demanding, daily choice, will lead us to marriage that happily lasts a lifetime.

It was a sweet moment.

I've grown concerned in recent years that more emphasis and certainly more time and money are spent preparing for the *wedding* than for the marriage. I'm certain God meant the ceremony to be a declaration and celebration of two becoming one in a lifelong commitment. But the dress and the cake have taken center stage and often seem more important than understanding the terms of the covenant. *And the covenant is what the wedding is really about.*

God holds us to the commitments made in a covenant, which is defined as a pledge between two parties. And because marriage was his idea, he has strong opinions about how the marriage covenant is to be treated. "'Til death do us part" does not mean *Until I'm tired of this relationship* or *Until it gets too difficult.* Pledging ourselves in marriage makes us subject to covenant commitment, not contractual conditions.

"For this reason a man shall leave his father and mother and be joined to his wife, and the two shall become one flesh," says Ephesians 5:31 (NKJV). God sees married couples as one: united, unified. The word in many translations for "joined" is *cleave*, which in the Hebrew means "to adhere or to stick to like glue." In other words, something that should not easily come apart or be separated.

Sadly, the divorce rate in the church is keeping pace with the statistics of nonbelievers. So what is the secret for honoring the marriage covenant all the days of our lives? *Commitment.*

H. Wallace Goddard, professor of Family Life at the University of Arkansas, has identified three levels of commitment in marriage, drawing from the work of J. M. Adams and W. H. Jones. Let's evaluate where you might be as we explore them.

1. *"Want to"* commitment. This is how people end up with a big white dress and a fancy suit at the altar. This commitment is based on desire and interest. The feelings of closeness and love that brought the couple to the marriage hold them there, fully satisfied.

2. *"Ought to"* commitment. Spouses may remain in an unhappy marriage out of a sense of duty or an unwillingness to break a vow they consider holy. Commitment becomes a struggle as they try to balance their feelings of dissatisfaction with the duty to remain.

3. *"Have to"* commitment. Often the presence of children or the feared disapproval of society holds people together. It may seem safer to remain in the relationship than to risk the financial consequences or loss of friends or family that a divorce might bring. The relationship must be endured.

So how do we achieve and sustain the satisfying *want to* commitment based on closeness and love? We choose it. Daily.

When Ron and I married, our commitment was once and only once: divorce was not an option. We vowed not to throw the *D* word around carelessly in anger or frustration or to threaten divorce in a season of difficulty or hardship. When that's the plan, you don't waste time when it's broken—you get to fixing it as quickly as possible.

That may not be the deal you were making the day you married, but it's a commitment you can choose today. Here are four important methods for staying committed.

1. *Get your priorities straight.* There is a God-designed order for our lives: God is first, you are second, and your spouse is third. Then come children, extended family, the church, and your job or ministry. Surprised you come before your spouse (and everyone else)? This is not a permission slip for selfishness. If we don't love and care for ourselves, we are unable to love anyone else. Guard your commitment by maintaining God's order.

2. *Evaluate your calendar.* We tend to get busy and commit time and energy to all sorts of activities. Even though they may be worthwhile pursuits, if they take away significant time with your spouse, examine them carefully. You may need to minimize or eliminate some.

3. *Have the big conversations.* We squabble too often about the same things over and over without exploring what lies beneath. Don't settle for the quick fix—get to the foundational issues that create commitment problems. Discuss, dig, and deal with it. Get help if needed from your pastor or a counselor.

4. *Don't despair during difficult times.* Hardships and stressful seasons shine a light on marriage and the small cracks become evident when lit. This is a gift. When the light comes on, the darkness must flee. Use those times to identify areas for attention and take action to strengthen your commitment. Enroll in a class at church, join a Bible study, pray and study the Word together. God created marriage; God has the answers.

If we build our lives together on feelings alone, we will fail. Marriage at its very best always requires much more. True commitment, which is an active, demanding, daily *choice*, will lead us to marriage that happily lasts a lifetime.

Conventional wisdom: "When asked how they managed to stay together for sixty-five years, the wife replied, 'We were born in a time where, if something was broken, you fixed it . . . you didn't throw it away.'"
—UNKNOWN

Chapter 6 Choice Questions:
I Choose to Keep My Commitment to You

1. What distractions demand time and attention that might communicate that your spouse is not a priority? What can you set aside?

2. Are your priorities in line with God's Word? Have you placed your kids, work, friends, or hobbies above the one with whom you are *one*? What can you do to realign them?

3. How can you demonstrate your commitment to your spouse and to your marriage?

Use the prayer below to declare your choice—or create one of your own.

Prayer: Father, I am committed to you and to your plan for my marriage. I ask you to daily strengthen my commitment to my spouse and my covenant pledge. I will align my life, my time, and my affection with your order for marriage, ensuring my spouse the place you've designed for him/her in my life. Make us unafraid to engage in the big conversations and reinforce our relationship as we submit our issues and needs to you. I will choose my marriage on easy days and difficult ones, based on my commitment to my spouse and to you, Lord. Thank you for your faithfulness to us and for calling us to a life of love and intimacy as a covenant couple.

CHAPTER 7

I CHOOSE TO BE LOYAL TO YOU

Many people will say that they are loyal, but who can find a reliable person?
—PROVERBS 20:6

He was the chancellor at a small but prestigious university; she, a beloved professor of dance. Theirs was a home overflowing with the conversation of students who never seemed to tire of their company. It was a satisfying life, and the couple felt genuinely blessed.

It started with missed appointments and words she couldn't easily find in conversation. They chalked it up to middle-aged memory. But the day she decided to clean out her closet, completely forgetting an important dress rehearsal for a major performance, they began to wonder if it might be something more. It was.

At only fifty-two, Shelby's doctor delivered the heartbreaking news that she was manifesting symptoms of early-onset

Alzheimer's—a rare form of the disease that inflicts only 5 percent of Alzheimer's victims. It starts early and moves quickly. She and her husband, Langdon, were stunned.

I became aware of their story more than fifteen years ago through a documentary on this cruel disease. The couple committed to continue what they had done all their lives—educate others. The film chronicled Shelby's life over several years. She resigned her position less than a year after her diagnosis, when it was clear she could not continue to drive. Destinations eluded her. She would wander in the car for hours, frantically at times, searching out something familiar.

In less than two years Langdon retired from his university post to care for his wife. He delighted in taking her out on a specially designed bicycle built for two so Shelby could enjoy the outdoors. Her laughter as the wind blew her hair around her face gave him all the energy he needed to push the pedals. As her condition declined, Langdon spent his days feeding her. Washing her hair. Changing her diapers.

Loyalty's not based on your feelings in the moment. It requires doing what you said you'd do, long after the mood you said it in has gone.

"She was slipping away from me, but occasionally I could see Shelby in there, in her eyes. And I'm certain she knows who I am," he said firmly.

The final scene in their story is one I'll never forget, although I watched it many years ago. Two folding chairs on a bare stage. One for Langdon and one for his and Shelby's adult daughter. She is crying, begging him to hear her. "Daddy, you've given up your life. Your work, your friends, everything. You've done more than most husbands would ever have attempted."

Her father takes her hand, patting it. "She needs care, Gwen. I want to make sure she has everything she needs."

"She *can* be cared for. But it's time. You need to let her go. There are wonderful places specializing in Alzheimer's. We can be sure she'll get care. Great care."

"I cannot do that," he says quietly.

"She doesn't even know who you are anymore, Daddy!" Gwen sobs and covers her face.

Langdon turns to Gwen, tucks his finger beneath her chin, and raises it to look into her eyes. He smiles. "Ah, you're right, sweet Gwennie girl; she doesn't." He pauses. "But I know who she is."

Right there, I remember thinking, *That's what I want in my marriage. Someone who knows who I am, even if I'm no longer certain myself. That's a loyalty that lives forever.*

Loyalty is not easy to come by. Even the Bible acknowledges this. Loyalty often comes at a cost, and it's not a value we discuss often in our culture.

We are not likely to be loyal to a new friend or casual acquaintance, but we should be able to assume loyalty to and from our spouse. Rabbi Barbara Penzner, co-founder of the Greater Boster Interfaith Organization, calls it "love across time." In other words, it's a result of shared experience with our mate over the period of our lives together.

One who is loyal might be described as devoted, constant, steadfast, faithful, dependable, reliable, or true. Those are big shoes to fill. It's not always convenient or even comfortable to be devoted. To remain so when the crowd moves the other direction may isolate you. Shifting loyalties has become a common way of coping with a shaky marriage. When couples stand at the altar with Plan B in mind, loyalty will not come easily, if it comes at all.

What does loyalty require?

- Consistent action.
- Determined decision.
- Dependable behavior.

It's a choice. It's *always* a choice.

Remember, to be loyal requires a behavioral choice; it is *demonstrated* in your words and actions and is reflected in your character. It's something visible, observable.

Here are some ideas to make sure your spouse knows where you stand.

- Speak positively about your spouse at all times. Don't talk behind his back to your girlfriends or to your mother about his shortcomings. Avoid complaining to the guys about her and don't try to round up a posse to agree with you *against* her.
- When you disagree with a decision or the behavior of your mate, have that conversation. But have it privately.
- Be reliable, even to the point of self-sacrifice. To receive loyalty, you must be willing to give it.
- Stick together, whatever may come at you. An "I will be there for you" or a "We're in this together" attitude will bond you and can bolster your mate's resolve and courage.
- Being loyal does not mean you'll always agree; neither does it require you to be blind or deaf to your spouse's foibles

and flaws. It means you help him develop and grow rather than stab him in the back or complain about her to others.

The choice to remain loyal cannot be based on how you feel in the moment. Peter was certain he would stay the course with Christ; he couldn't imagine denying him. But in the moment, when the pressure came, the disciple's loyalty waivered. Perhaps not in his heart, but in his actions. Commitment means staying true to what you said you would do, long after the mood you said it in has left. Everyone deserves such confidence.

I'm certain there were days Langdon felt he couldn't continue to care for his beloved Shelby. The film ended before her life did. Did he remain determined to care for her himself? We don't know for sure, but my money's on Langdon. For others, placement with caring medical professionals would be tough but best. Loyalty is about making the choice to remain reliable and faithful with the best interest of the other person guiding the decision.

What about loyalty to *your* mate? What will you choose today?

> *Conventional wisdom: "When it comes to relationships, remaining faithful is never an option, but a priority. Loyalty is everything."*
>
> —UNKNOWN

Chapter 7 Choice Questions:
I Choose to Be Loyal to You

1. How would your mate describe your loyalty to him or her? Describe how well the following words fit your actions and behavior: *dependable, faithful, true, reliable, steadfast, constant, devoted*?

2. What struggles have you experienced in the past with regard to demonstrating loyalty to your spouse? What will you need to do to reverse that trend and overcome the challenges?

3. Starting today, how will you choose to communicate your loyalty to your spouse?

Use the prayer below to declare your choice—or create one of your own.

Prayer: You, dear Lord, are the most loyal of all. Your commitment to us is unwavering, as evidenced when you sent us your Son, Jesus. I desire to be loyal to my husband/wife and to build true understanding of my allegiance in his/her heart. Help me to be consistent in my behavior and to follow through so there is no question of my love and loyalty. Father, when I am tempted to shift my commitment, remind me of your example, so that I am known by my spouse and by all others as faithful and devoted.

CHAPTER 8

I CHOOSE TO TRUST YOU

Love puts up with all things, trusts in all things, hopes for all things, endures all things.

—1 CORINTHIANS 13:7

"This was not an easy call to make," said the woman on the phone, "but I thought you deserved to know."

The caller was from our church. "Oh my goodness, Sherri. What's wrong?"

She didn't respond immediately, and then she said, "I think your husband has a thing for me."

"A *thing*? What kind of thing? What are you talking about?"

"I think Ron's attracted to me. I think he's interested in me romantically." She sounded out of breath, nervous.

Sherri was several years younger than Ron and me, married with two toddlers. Blonde, slender, and attractive, she was also a troubled person.

I took a deep breath. "Tell me why you think Ron is interested in you, Sherri. What has happened to make you feel this way?"

"Well…" she said slowly. "Nothing's actually happened. I just feel it when I see him or when we talk."

"Has he said or done anything that you consider inappropriate? Anything that made you uncomfortable?" I already knew the answer.

"No," she responded. "But a woman just knows these things."

Ron and I had been guests in Sherri and Bob's home, but we were not close friends. As the directors of our church's marriage ministry, we spent time with couples, often in groups and occasionally with a couple for dinner or coffee. That was the extent of our relationship with Sherri and her husband other than church attendance and activities.

Sherri seemed to have little confidence in her marriage. "Bob works with a lot of women. It really bugs me," she once said in a women's Sunday school class. She also disliked Bob's close relationship with his sister and was bothered by their frequent phone calls.

"I'm not sure what you're sensing, Sherri, but I *am* sure you are wrong," I countered. "Perhaps you've mistaken his friendliness for something more personal." Ron was a side-hugger with women other than family, for crying out loud. This is a man I know. This is a man I trust.

Trust is built over time, with consistent, transparent behavior that honors God and the marriage commitment.

Sherri was insistent. "No. I know what I feel. There's definitely something there."

"Sherri," I said quietly, "I think *you* might be experiencing feelings for Ron and can't quite acknowledge it. It must be uncomfortable for you to realize you are drawn to a man other than Bob."

The couple had previously shared their marital challenges openly with us. Their relationship had become difficult and Sherri was unhappy, although neither she nor Bob could identify the cause of her dissatisfaction. And sadly, men in ministry like Ron often become a fixation for women in this situation. Pastors seem like the perfect mate: godly, caring, and compassionate. Ron's a really great guy, but I know he's not perfect. I also knew he didn't have a thing for Sherri.

"I thought you needed to know, that's all," she concluded. And with that, she hung up.

How could I be so certain? Why did I choose to trust my husband?

Ron had a good track record with me—his behavior over the years of our relationship has been consistent. I've prayed with him, worshiped alongside him, and counseled others with him. I know his heart. He's honored our marriage, and he's *earned* my trust.

I could have set aside my positive experiences and all that I know about him and been suspicious. I could have grilled Sherri for more details and given Ron the third degree when he got home. I chose to trust him instead.

A mate who has earned trust, is due trust.

Sometimes, mistrust is not about the other person at all. It's a lack of confidence in *oneself*. My own insecurities could have triggered a landslide of fear when the phone rang. Satan's goal was to tempt me to doubt my husband and create division in our relationship, even though my experience with Ron was sound.

It would have been incredibly unfair, but the enemy never plays fair.

Marriage without trust is miserable. Trust is an outcome of life experience built with your spouse. If it's been broken through infidelity, dishonesty, or other damaging behavior, it's next to impossible to simply set aside the hurt and extend trust immediately. If you are the offending party, it's not reasonable to expect it to come instantly or easily. Trust must be earned back, *over time*, with consistent, transparent behavior that honors God and the marriage commitment. If you are the one betrayed, and you choose to remain in the marriage, you must *choose* to trust again, allowing your spouse the opportunity to rebuild your faith in him or her. Constant cross-examination or doubt when there is no evidence to support it has the potential to destroy the relationship.

I encourage you to examine your heart right now. What insecurities plague you? The enemy will whisper accusation and attempt to leverage those insecurities against your marriage. Refuse to let him shatter the trust you've built as a couple.

Our senior pastor met with Sherri and her husband; both men were stunned. During their discussion, she acknowledged she had a crush on my husband, and eventually she apologized to us. My heart hurt for her. She was unhappy, confused, and now embarrassed beyond belief. For someone already struggling with insecurity, this didn't help.

I was right to trust Ron. I am grateful to have made that choice.

The *Amplified Bible* translates 1 Corinthians 13:7 beautifully: "Love bears up under anything and everything that comes, is *ever ready to believe the best of every person*, its hopes are fadeless under all circumstances, and it endures everything" (emphasis mine).

Today, what will you do when faced with a dilemma of trust? It's always a choice.

> *Conventional Wisdom: "It takes years to build up trust, and it only takes suspicion, not proof, to destroy it."*
> —UNKNOWN

Chapter 8 Choice Questions:
I Choose to Trust You

1. What challenges the trust level in your marriage? What experiences, issues, or insecurities make it difficult to trust?
2. When are you tempted to withhold trust in your relationship? Why?
3. How will you choose today to demonstrate trust in your spouse?

Use the prayer below to declare your choice—or create one of your own.

Prayer: Father, marriage without trust is not the life you desire for us. I recognize that trusting others requires vulnerability that may not always be easy or comfortable for me. I choose to trust my spouse, knowing that to do so is better than to live with unfounded suspicion. If I've been deceived by my mate, and he/she has repented, I choose to allow him or her to rebuild the broken trust. I will not allow my spouse's past dishonesty to blind me to covenant behavior when it is demonstrated, and I will not allow the enemy to tempt me to needlessly distrust. I have fully forgiven broken trust, and today I choose to believe the best in my mate.

CHAPTER 9

I CHOOSE TO FORGIVE YOU

Be kind, compassionate, and forgiving to each other, in the
same way God forgave you in Christ.
—EPHESIANS 4:32

It came as a devastating blow. She never suspected. Perhaps she should have recognized the signs, but who could believe he'd cheat on her? And with their employee, who just happened to be her good friend. It never crossed her mind as a possibility. Not after all these years, the kids, the business. *What did I miss?*

Nothing. I didn't miss anything, she told herself. *There were no clues. I wonder if the old saying is true: once a cheater, always a cheater?* The prospect was more than her mind could handle.

Gary and Mona had been married nineteen years when he confessed a long-running affair. "I felt like such a fool," Mona told me. "Her marriage was troubled. My kids were a challenge. We joked that I had the happy marriage and she had the happy kids. How on earth did she keep a straight face? She must have been laughing behind my back the entire time."

That it happened at all was heartbreaking. That it involved a woman Mona loved and had included in her life for a few years was shattering. They were best friends, or so she had thought.

Gary had confessed it all to his pastor, and then to Mona. He was remorseful and didn't want a divorce. He told Mona he'd never stopped loving her. Said he'd do whatever it would take to make it through this. Mona didn't know what she wanted, but they had three boys and she felt like she had to at least try. And the woman would no longer be employed in their business.

Forgiveness means I value you and the relationship more than holding on to the anger or the hurt you caused. I forgive you because I choose you.

Mona couldn't find a good reason to refuse rebuilding the marriage. Through counseling and hard work, she recognized there were things they both could have done to sustain a healthier relationship before the affair. Stepping out of his marriage vows was a choice Gary made; nothing excused it, and he accepted full responsibility for his behavior. But he and his wife both learned a lot about how and why this had happened. Then he asked the question Mona struggled to answer: "Will you forgive me?"

Forgiveness is a choice. Always. And it can be a difficult choice.

Gary and Mona experienced one of the greatest assaults a marriage may experience. But forgiveness can be a challenge over far less than adultery.

- Secret overspending, running up the credit cards.
- A private *guys' night out* disguised as working late.

- An argument over him leaving her with an empty gas tank—again.
- Her correcting him in front of her family or in front of his coworkers at the Christmas party.

Betrayal, broken trust, or just garden-variety conflict. Each requires a decision about how you will choose to handle it. For the Christ follower, forgiveness is the obvious choice, whether you feel like forgiving or not.

Conflict requires two participants willing to keep the discord and misery alive. At any time, either party can make a choice. One may seek forgiveness or the other may forgive, whether it's requested or not. "Where *there is* no wood, the fire goes out; And where *there is* no talebearer, strife ceases" (Proverbs 26:20 NKJV).

Forgiving one who has hurt you or angered you doesn't mean *you win* or *I'm wrong*. It means I value *you* and the *relationship* more than holding on to the anger or the hurt. I forgive you because I choose you. It's not easy to do, but it's what the Word instructs, and God promises that when we stop adding fuel to the fire, it dies. Things may not be resolved— there are probably still hurt feelings and wounds to deal with, stuff to work out. But forgiveness begins a process. The process takes time, though with the heat turned down, you can work it out together. Forgiveness doesn't change what happened in the past, but it can enlarge the possibilities of your future.

There are few topics in the Bible that are as clear about God's direction as what you will find on forgiveness. Here are some reminders:

- *Be prepared to forgive.* Forgiveness is not a microwavable solution; it may need to be repeated, often, and sometimes for the same issue. "Then Peter came to him and asked, 'Lord, how often should I forgive someone who sins against me? Seven times?' 'No, not seven times,' Jesus replied, 'but seventy times seven!'" (Matthew 18:21-22 NLT).

- *Forgiveness has nothing to do with justice.* Forgiving is an action that frees *you* from being controlled by your anger, your hurt, or your past. You may feel as though your spouse doesn't deserve your forgiveness, but remember, we didn't get from Jesus what we deserved; we received what *he* deserved—freedom from sin and death, a place in the family of God, and a life redeemed.

- *Forgive out of obedience to God.* "Bear with each other and forgive one another if any of you has a grievance against someone. Forgive as the Lord forgave you" (Colossians 3:13 NIV). Forgiving others isn't a suggestion; it's a critical component of life in Christ. When we withhold forgiveness, we are in direct disobedience to God's Word.

- *Unforgiveness damages you.* As the old saying goes, refusing to forgive is like drinking poison and waiting for the other person to die. "And when you stand praying, if you hold anything against anyone, forgive them, so that your Father in heaven may forgive you your sins" (Mark 11:25 NIV). Our relationship with God is impacted when we reject his call to forgive.

Mona rejected the idea of divorce and realized that only by forgiving Gary could God begin to heal their marriage. They made their way back slowly, through counseling and prayer. Out of their pain, the Lord birthed something beautiful—a ministry to help others floundering in the sea of infidelity (they can be contacted through their ministry website: www.hopeand healing.us). Countless couples have seen their marriages restored by the counsel and teaching God has provided through Mona and Gary.

Ruth Bell Graham said it best: "A good marriage is the union of two forgivers.... You're going to hurt one another over and over again during your lifetime together. If you don't know how to ask for forgiveness and give forgiveness, you're never going to have a great marriage."

Do you want a great marriage? Of course you do! So...what will you choose today?

> *Conventional wisdom: "The first to apologize is the bravest. The first to forgive is the strongest. The first to forget is the happiest."*
>
> —Unknown

Chapter 9 Choice Questions: I Choose to Forgive You

1. How easily do you and your spouse forgive one another? What prevents forgiveness or promotes it in your relationship?

2. Had you ever considered the impact of withholding forgiveness? Look up the following scriptures and record what you learn: Matthew 6:14-15; Mark 11:25; Luke 6:37; 2 Corinthians 2:7; Philippians 3:13-14.

3. What will you need to do to forgive your spouse when your feelings don't fall in line with God's direction?

Use the prayer below to declare your choice—or create one of your own.

Prayer: Father, thank you for Jesus, through whom I have forgiveness for every sin I have ever committed and every sin I will ever commit. His blood covers it all. You did not wait until I deserved forgiveness; there is nothing I could ever do that would be sufficient. You provided the sacrifice to forgive my sin because you love me. Guide me by your Spirit to follow your example of grace when I must forgive my husband/wife. I choose to forgive when I don't feel like it, when he/she doesn't deserve it, and even when my spouse hasn't asked for it. I choose to do it because I love you and my desire is obedience to your Word— without delay. I believe my obedience will provide the path to restore what was broken and allow us to move together toward your desire for our life together.

CHAPTER 10

I CHOOSE TO BE
ADAPTABLE

There's a season for everything and a time for every matter under the heavens.

—Ecclesiastes 3:1

The only person who really likes change is a wet baby.

I'm fairly sure my mother didn't originate that line, but I've never heard it anywhere else. For years, it summed up my feelings about change. I'm aware that adaptability is greatly prized; it's a tremendous asset in business, and *going with the flow* helps you stay sane in a rapidly paced world. *I get it.* I struggle with it nonetheless. I'm better than I once was, but let's agree: it's not my gift.

I was born late in my parents' lives. My only sibling was sixteen and none too thrilled with my arrival. By the time I was two, he was away at college and never lived at home again. Mom said it was like raising two only children. He got their youth and health. I got their stability.

From birth to the day I married, I lived in one state, in one town, in one house. I was never the new kid on the block, the new kid at church, or the new kid at school. I showed the new kids around. Safe. Comfortable. Nice. As a result, change does not come easily for me. Because it was not my experience in my formative years, I typically make another selection when change is on the menu.

I like things the way I like them. Oh, so do you, just admit it. But I can be rather insistent on how I think things should go—or so it has been suggested. I've become more aware of this in recent years as the number of pointer-outers in my life has increased, and God has joined them in bringing it to my attention. *Don't insist on your own way* is the clear message.

As our circumstances in life shift, adaptability is required to deal successfully with change. We must be willing to let go of, and sometimes even grieve for, *what was* to allow us to pursue *what can be*. It requires us to be open to growth and influence rather than staying stuck in our own preferences, sometimes called a comfort zone. Inflexibility can easily cause us to become alienated from others who move on. And those who stay behind, out of loyalty or a sense of duty to accommodate us, find their lives miserable in the process.

> *As life changes, we must adapt. When we let go of what was, we can pursue what can be.*

Marriage itself brings massive change. There's another person with different experiences, ideas, preferences, and approaches that cannot be automatically dismissed. You realize this is not Burger King—you can't always have it your way. You can try, but it's not the best approach to a healthy marriage. Even if you can make your case and push your preference through, resentment may build in the heart of your partner and, over time, erode unity and agreement.

Once we marry, we can no longer call the shots on our own if we desire a vibrant partnership where each has a voice. We must be flexible.

Never did I anticipate the number or variety of changes God would bring into our lives as a couple and as parents. Yet as he has so often done, when the Lord teaches me a principle, he provides opportunities for practice.

- Ron and I lived nontraditional roles in our marriage. He stayed home with our sons and ran his business from there for eighteen years while my career took me on the road.
- God moved Ron into full-time ministry after twenty-nine years of marriage—a change that shifted much of the financial responsibility to me.
- Lifelong Californians, the Lord directed us to relocate to Texas in 2004, leaving our entire family behind. (It's okay. Nearly all of them have joined us here.)

I'd be lying if I said it was simple. But throughout our lives we've had this consistent experience with God: what he orders, he pays for. In other words, when we are obedient, he makes the way.

Although my husband and I have personally come face-to-face with the need for adaptability, God has provided some amazing biblical examples of saints navigating change. What if Moses had refused to accept the charge to lead the Israelites out of Egypt? Or if Noah had decided he wasn't into boat building?

What if David had taken Saul's armor rather than the slingshot and five smooth stones? Even Mary, though troubled by the visit of the angel, proclaimed in Luke 1:38: "I am the Lord's servant. Let it be with me as you have said." Each person made a choice to let go of a program already in progress and adapt to God's direction. Each time, God was faithful.

Change can come in big packages, as in *giving birth to the Son of God*, or in small ones: "Look, honey, I rearranged the living room furniture!" For those who struggle, change can create pandemonium regardless of the magnitude. Here are a few tips for flexing up:

- *Keep prayer at the forefront.* I'm not talking about one of those *Please don't make me do this* prayers. Ask God to give you and your spouse both a common understanding of the change *and* shared direction on what to do. Not hearing clearly? Ask trusted believers in your life to pray for you. God spoke through a donkey to deliver a message (Numbers 22:28); he can certainly get a message to you.

- *Keep the big picture in mind.* What has God directed for your lives together? What are you *already* clear about? We knew God wanted Ron in full-time ministry, but moving to Texas was a surprise. It made sense once we stepped back for the long view. The lower cost of living and additional connections God created for us pointed to the Lone Star State. In fact, we'd have missed what God called us to do had we resisted this change.

- *Keep things in perspective.* If it's not a big deal, don't make it a big deal. I remember hearing my dad often ask my mom as we headed downtown to dine out, "Dot, what would you like to eat tonight?" Most of the time, Mom's response was, "I don't care, Larry. Whatever you want." Sounds flexible, right? "Well then, I'd like Chinese food," was his favorite response. "Oh, *you* don't want Chinese!" she'd exclaim. Of course he did; it was rarely *her* choice. This always made me laugh. They laughed too. Mom ate more chow mein than she preferred, and Dad often deferred to Italian. Married for fifty-four years, they'd learned to be flexible and keep it all in perspective.

Change is inevitable. God wants us to prepare and plan for our lives as we submit to his will. There is, however, a Yiddish saying based on Proverbs 19:21: "Man plans and God laughs." I'm not sure God is laughing, but I do know the Lord's plan and purpose are what I want in my marriage, even if I have to Gumby up to get there!

How about you? What will you choose today?

Conventional wisdom: "Blessed are the flexible, for they shall not break!"
—UNKNOWN

Chapter 10 Choice Questions:
I Choose to Be Adaptable

1. What are your experiences with change? Love it? Resist it? How about your spouse? Similar or very different?
2. How flexible do you need to be in your relationship with your spouse? Is that mutual? Do you both adapt to one another as needed?
3. Which of the tips listed in this chapter would be helpful to extend your ability to flex and deal with change in your marriage? What will you do to implement it?

Use the prayer below to declare your choice—or create one of your own.

Prayer: Lord, I see the examples in your Word of men and women who adapted their lives to your will and purpose. I desire my marriage to reflect you in everything I do personally and in all we do as a couple. I surrender my need to have it my way and ask for your help to be flexible in my relationship with my spouse. I pray we grow together in unity as we allow you to establish our path to that goal. Today, I choose to bend like a willow tree to the wind of your will.

CHAPTER 11

I CHOOSE TO SUBMIT
TO YOU

*Always give thanks to God the Father for everything in the
name of our Lord Jesus Christ; and submit to each other out of
respect for Christ.*

—EPHESIANS 5:20-21

Did you see the reviews on that new movie we've been waiting for? The one we've been talking about?" my daughter-
in-law asked me. "I was kind of surprised; I heard..."

"Me too!" I cut in. "I was really disappointed, because it
sounded so promising, something we'd all really like," I continued. "The film got really low marks in several areas, like..."

Ron gave me a nudge with his knee.

I glanced at him without comment and continued, "The
reviews I read said it really plodded along and was hard to follow
at times. And such a predictable ending . . ."

He nudged me again. I turned to face him and he gave me *the
look*, along with *another* nudge.

I rolled my eyes at him. But I stopped talking and turned my attention to Penny. "What did you hear?" I asked her. She was eager to tell me.

The next morning, as we lay in bed contemplating the jump from the warmth of the comforter into the start of our day, Ron said to me, "So, did you understand why I nudged your knee last night?"

"Yeah, I got it; I interrupted her and hijacked the conversation. Thanks. You were right. Irritating, but right."

He laughed; I smiled. That's how it works most often. After practicing for nearly forty years, that's where we usually land. *Usually.* Still, there are times it's not easy.

I will admit the concept of submitting to each other was a tough pill to swallow when we married at nineteen. Ron and I are both strong willed, opinionated, and unafraid to express ourselves. On occasion, it has resulted in what we call *an intense moment of fellowship.* Sometimes it's been loud. But neither of us will ever be able to say to the other, "Wow! I didn't know you felt that way!"

There have been occasions when our spirited debate crossed the line and our expression of love and respect slipped—times when neither of us would yield to the other. On those occasions, we had to seek forgiveness from one another, and from God as well.

Submission can be tough. It has been discussed a great deal throughout the life of the church. I've heard some really excellent messages about it, and some that weren't so great. And by *not great*, I mean they weren't based in Scripture.

The Bible is clear: we are to submit to one another. Early on, God said it was not good for man to be alone; he needed a help meet. The word for *help meet* in the Hebrew of Genesis 2:18 (KJV) is used nineteen additional times in the Bible, all in reference to "aid in battle"—aid that usually came from God. Standing with your spouse against the attacks of the enemy to establish and protect your marriage is an important role. And it's always a choice.

God created a specific pattern for marriage so that disputes are never left undecided or one-sided: "Wives, submit to your own husbands as you do to the Lord" (Ephesians 5:22 NIV). "Husbands, love your wives, just as Christ loved the church and gave himself up for her" (Ephesians 5:25 NIV). God placed the husband at the head of the home, a position not to exalt him but to *create order.* My mother would say that anything with two heads is a monster. I've seen husbands and wives vie for headship in marriage, battling for top spot, and it's not pretty. Often the monster devours the marriage, or even if the union is not dissolved, peace and unity vanish.

Standing with your spouse against the attacks of the enemy to establish and protect your marriage is an important role. And it's always a choice.

God established the order: my husband is to love me (as Christ loved the church), and he is held accountable as the head of the home. That's God's plan, not my husband's. If I am submitted to the Lord, I will submit to his plan. It doesn't mean I have no input in decisions or the direction for our life together.

"I don't want a servant for a wife," Ron says. "A silent partner might work in business, but it's not helpful in marriage. I need a wife who will pray with and for me, offer insights and ideas, and share her heart as God leads her. I want a partner in making decisions. God knows me, and the world should not be exposed to me without her influence!"

The concept of yielding to one another has become important in our marriage. It ensures we each have a voice. Yielding is a voluntary process, a choice to agree to or accept something that you have been resisting or opposing. The choice to yield may come as a result of influence, position, affection, or respect for another.

There is a second meaning for this word: *yield* also describes the outcome or results of a choice or action. The farmer's careful oversight of his crop yields a fruitful harvest. Godly, biblical choices yield a productive and favorable outcome. Insisting on our own way and refusing to submit will produce an outcome too, though not one Ron and I would care to live with.

Sometimes I am able to influence his heart, and at times he has influenced mine through open, respectful dialogue. We submit to one another. Do we always find full and complete agreement on every topic? Of course not! In those instances, I choose to submit to God's plan and order and yield to my husband. After all, he will have to account to God for the choices he makes.

What will you choose when the opportunity to yield comes knocking? Will you resist the temptation to bully or campaign to get your own way? Will you demand submission? Or will you create dialogue to allow understanding? It's not always easy, but it's always a choice.

Conventional wisdom: "Submissive does not mean weakness. It is meekness, not weakness. It is strength under control. It is bridled control."
—CANDACE CAMERON BURE

Chapter 11 Choice Questions:
I Choose to Submit to You

1. What's your style when you or your spouse do not agree on a decision or course of action? What is the outcome of your approach?

2. Does your style honor your spouse? Does it honor God and his Word? Why or why not?

3. Have a conversation with your spouse to review your patterns:

   • Why is it important to submit to one another according to Ephesians 5:21?

   • How well do we submit to one another? What steps can we take to improve?

   • When there is a lack of agreement after dialogue, what choice will we make?

Use the prayer below to declare your choice—or create one of your own.

Prayer: Father, I yield to you and to your Word. I recognize that your instruction for husbands and wives is designed to create order in our marriage. When I choose to honor your Word, I am choosing to honor you *and* my spouse. I acknowledge that submitting to one another may sometimes be complicated, but all things are possible in you. Holy Spirit, I ask that you enable me to set aside pride, entitlement, and the need to have things my own way. I pray you will do the same in the heart of my spouse. Remind us in the moment to yield to one another, listening to understand, and offering our own insights and ideas in a respectful and loving way. Lord, please guide us as a couple to yield our hearts and minds to your will, your plan, and your order.

I CHOOSE TO SHARE
YOUR BURDENS

Carry each other's burdens, and in this way you will fulfill the law of Christ.
—GALATIANS 6:2 (NIV)

I can take care of your mom," he said.

It took me by surprise—not because it was the first time he'd offered his help, but because of the depth of care she now needed. These were her final weeks, we'd been told. She was ready, unafraid. But my once fiercely independent mother now required support with even the simplest of life's daily demands.

As a late-in-life baby, I had understood what it meant to provide help to aging parents long before I was an adult. The emergency room and ICU were familiar, though never comfortable for me. I could recite medical histories for both of my parents by age twelve and knew what symptoms to watch for. I reminded them about taking medication and doctor appointments. It wasn't difficult, and I never resented being thrown into what might be considered adult responsibilities so young, but it was quite different from the daily activities my friends were engaged in.

When Ron and I married, still teenagers, his caregiver education began. He learned about the world of late-night urgent phone calls and navigation of hospital corridors. We followed ambulances to the ER and listened to the pulse and throb of ICU monitors. He was always supportive and never complained. Not surprisingly, my folks loved him dearly—my mother could not have loved him more if he had been her own. It was a unique relationship.

When my dad died, seven years before we lost Mom, he asked Ron to take care of "my Dottie." Without hesitation Ron promised he would, although I'm not sure he knew exactly what that might entail when he made the commitment.

More quickly than I expected, we were there, nearing the end.

I was struggling with the pressure of caring for Mom and running my business, which had been back-burnered for nearly a month. Clients understood, but loss of both income and potential future opportunities was a genuine concern. Yet I wasn't sure Ron would be able to step in as the primary caregiver when he offered to do so.

"She needs help with *everything*, Ron," I reminded him. "She needs to be fed at times when she's really weak…and she needs help in the bathroom. Can you do that?"

"I will if she'll let me." My heart melted. "I love your mom like she was my own. She needs help. I can do this," he said firmly.

His willingness to share what had become a weighty responsibility—mentally, emotionally, and spiritually—communicated his love for me as no bouquet of roses ever could. Although Ron empathized with me, he went well beyond letting me know he understood how difficult this had become. He offered *real* assistance. Helping hands. He stepped in to lighten my load, to carry the weight of helping my mom move from this life to the next. I can't remember a time when I felt more cared for, more supported, *more loved*. My husband's commitment to share this responsibility changed how I saw him. It touched my heart and deepened my love for him in a way that's difficult to describe.

Sharing the mental, emotional and spiritual responsibility of a burden communicates your love for one another, as no other gift ever will.

"Carry each other's burdens, and in this way you will fulfill the law of Christ" (Galatians 6:2 NIV). Paul encourages us to gladly share the load of others, for it accomplishes what Jesus called the "new" commandment—to love one another.

Ron and I sat down with Mom, and he asked if she would allow him to serve her, stepping in as her primary caregiver when I had to be away from home. "I'm embarrassed to need so much help," she said, "but if you can live with it, son, so can I." And though it was a brief time, Ron cared for Mom in those weeks. He became Jesus with skin on, active and alive, his actions providing evidence of his love for her.

And for me.

Conventional wisdom: "Many hands lighten the load."
—UNKNOWN

Chapter 12 Choice Questions:
I Choose to Share Your Burdens

1. What issues, concerns, or responsibilities are weighing heavily on your spouse? Think about financial or family issues, health problems, challenges on the job. What are the signs or indicators that suggest he/she is struggling?

2. What can you choose to do, beginning today, to lighten the load for your spouse? How can you walk in Galatians 6:2 in this situation? Support can come in a variety of ways:

   • Physical support: hands on, as Ron provided to me.

   • Emotional support: empathizing, letting your spouse know you understand the situation he/she is dealing with and the impact it's having on him/her.

   • Mental support: offering to discuss the issue, acting as a sounding board, or brainstorming ways to overcome or minimize the impact of the situation.

   • Spiritual support: praying your spouse through the circumstances.

3. What can you do to make a difference? Be specific.

   • Mentally?

   • Emotionally?

   • Physically?

   • Spiritually?

Use the prayer below to declare your choice—or create one of your own.

Prayer: Father, you have commanded us to love one another—and to love not only in word, but in deed. Because the two of us have become one, the burden my spouse carries is mine as well. Please help me understand the best way to provide support in this challenge, and show me the ways that will provide the greatest relief and demonstration of my love. I ask for your strength that I may bless my spouse and honor you by fulfilling the law of Christ. Please guide me to do all of this with a glad heart and an attitude of love.

CHAPTER 13

I CHOOSE TO SERVE YOU

But the one who is greatest among you will be your servant.
—Matthew 23:11

I awakened slowly to sunlight streaming in through the sliding-glass doors. It took a moment for my eyes to adjust. *Where am I?* From the comfort of the leather recliner, I looked around the room, taking in the photos of sea turtles and the collection of shells on the coffee table. *Oh, right. Florida.* Vacation, beginning the first day of the new year. The last thing I recalled was sitting down in the comfy chair to look over the info our friends had left for us in their condo.

"Ron?" I called.

"In here." I made my way to the bedroom, where he was placing my shoes in the closet. I went to my suitcase lying closed on the foot of the bed. It was empty.

"How long have I been asleep?"

Ron looked at me and grinned. "A couple of hours, I think. You were *out.*" He placed the empty suitcase in the corner.

"You've been burning the candle at both ends for weeks. Guess you really needed to catch up on your rest."

He had unpacked. Everything. His *and* mine. Clothes, toiletries, shoes, books—all of it. Hung up in the closet, folded in drawers, my book on the nightstand.

"Why did you do that? You should have left it for me, or you could have wakened me."

He gave me a hug. "Nah. You were sleeping so peacefully, I didn't have the heart to interrupt. I just wanted to get it done so that when you woke up, we could go do something fun."

Ron knows how much I hate unpacking. Putting things *in* the suitcase is not a problem, but taking it all *out* and finding a place for it, I loathe. What a nice way to begin our time away together, with my sweet hubby's servant-heart in full swing.

Ron has a heart to serve. He's spent many years in ministry. His mom and his sisters, our sons and their families, have all been beneficiaries of his care and oversight. And he has always served me.

I've occasionally struggled to do the same for him. Or at least to do it cheerfully. Big difference. Ron actively seeks opportunities to serve me; I sometimes stumble onto serving him.

Serving my spouse should be mutual and without hesitation—an outcome of my commitment to follow Jesus. It shouldn't be based on convenience or the difficulty of the task or how I feel in the moment. It should simply *be*. "Work with enthusiasm, as though you were working for the Lord rather than for people" (Ephesians 6:7 NLT). I need that tattooed somewhere I can't miss it.

Author Ambrose Bierce said it like it is in his definition of marriage: "A community consisting of a master, a mistress, and two slaves, making in all, two." Bierce, an agnostic nicknamed "Bitter Bierce," recorded the definition in a satirical book, poking fun at matrimony. But he had it right: we are to serve one another.

Christ is our best example of demonstrating servanthood as God meant it to be. When we serve our spouse,

We demonstrate not only our love, but also God's love in the moment we choose to serve.

we access the opportunity to strengthen our relationship rather than just meeting his or her need. Relationship versus neediness. Giving versus getting. We demonstrate not only our love but also God's love in the moment we choose to serve. It makes our heavenly Father smile.

I'd like to make him smile more often. If I can make that happen while blessing my husband, it's a really great two-for-one deal!

Service won't always be a big event. It might be as simple as picking up his dry cleaning or gassing up the car for her because she hates doing it. Helping him host his friends for a Super Bowl party with you as head chef and snack supplier. Driving her to the airport and picking her up so she doesn't have to struggle with her bags or remember where she parked the car after a trip. Service helps send the message: I choose you today. Whether it's easy or convenient or messy. I choose to serve you.

Some quick tips on serving your spouse:

- *Anticipate the opportunity to serve.* What's happening in your mate's life at the moment? Big project at work? Ministry opportunity? Major presentation at the corporate office? Look ahead and fill the need without waiting for the request.

- *Do it cheerfully.* Service in some areas of our lives may fall under the heading of obligation, but it can still be done with a positive attitude and a smile on our face. Nothing hollers, "Love you!" like serving your mate eagerly.
- *Ask how you might serve.* Sometimes the need is not obvious. Some people don't like to ask for help. Give your spouse a chance to let you in on service opportunities. Ask: "What are your goals this week?" "How can I help you accomplish them?" "Is there anything I can do to make it easier for you?"

With the suitcases unpacked and things put away, Ron and I could explore that "something fun" he'd mentioned. We glanced at the ocean glistening outside. It beckoned; we answered. Is there anything better than beach-walking with your baby? Not as far as I know.

So, what will you choose? How will you serve today?

Conventional wisdom: "The only way we can serve God on earth is by serving others."
—RICK WARREN

Chapter 13 Choice Questions:
I Choose to Serve You

1. What do you do to serve your spouse? Do you serve naturally, or is it always an intentional choice when you do it?
2. What ideas or scriptures stood out to you most in this chapter?
3. What's your plan to use what you've learned? What will you do to serve your spouse?

Use the prayer below to declare your choice—or create one of your own.

Prayer: Father, your Word says: "For even the Son of Man came not to be served but to serve others and to give his life as a ransom for many" (Matthew 20:28 NLT). As in all things, Jesus is our example. I ask you to help me see the opportunities in my mate's life to serve, and to serve with a glad heart. Holy Spirit, prompt me to notice when my spouse is in need of my help—when the load is heavy and an extra hand would provide relief. Give me the desire to bless him or her, and the grace to serve without complaint. Whether it's a large task or something small, I choose to demonstrate the love of Christ and serve my loved one today.

CHAPTER 14

I CHOOSE TO BE GENEROUS WITH YOU

Tell them to do good, to be rich in the good things they do, to be generous, and to share with others.
—1 Timothy 6:18

W hat a husband! I realized I'd made a mistake when I bought a new desktop computer—what would I use when we traveled? My netbook was out of date, but cheap me refused to buy another laptop. I'm typing this status on my brand-new Christmas present—a new laptop. I'm so blessed to have a husband who supports my writing."

My Facebook friend who wrote this is an author who relies on her computer. Her husband saw an opportunity to bless his wife and generously reached into his treasury to make it happen. It's not your typical surprise of roses and candy. It's better! It's better because it's specific to his wife's need.

Then there was the time husbands Tom, Curtis, and Ron prepared a fabulous gourmet meal for a houseful of women on a weekend retreat. Their wives were among those in attendance, but all of the women commented on the generous gift of time the three had given to bless the group. The fact they also cleaned the kitchen afterward was a double blessing indeed!

My husband is a student of the Word of God. A serious student. For years I've watched him spend hours with his concordance, commentaries, and Bible spread out over his desk as he researches a passage or prepares a message. His intimate knowledge of the Bible amazes me. As a Christian writer, I often consult with Ron to help me understand a nuance of Scripture or to locate a passage that I know is there but cannot find. And when he needs help as he writes out a message, I am available to edit, brainstorm, or polish. We each generously share our knowledge and talent.

Time. Talent. Treasure. Three areas for generosity. Three distinct opportunities to invest in your husband or wife.

- "Get the upgrade to first class, babe. It's only forty dollars. You're exhausted, and it's been a long week."
- "You're heading out on that trip soon. You need to replace your old backpack. I saw some I think would work well."
- "Let me show you an easier way to do that…"
- "Sure, I can take the time to drive you down to the conference."

A generous heart blesses both the giver and the receiver. The Bible promises there is a return on the investment we make: "Give, and you will receive. Your gift will return to you in full—pressed down, shaken together to make room for more, running over, and poured into your lap. The amount you give will determine the amount you get back" (Luke 6:38 NLT). In other words, you can't outgive God.

The principle holds true whether you give your time, talent, or treasure. I may have a limited budget and can't surprise my husband with that new camera he's been looking at. But giving him my undivided attention when he needs it to discuss a difficult situation at work or a concern about his aging mother is far more valuable in the moment. It meets a specific, immediate need.

God's investment strategy is clear: when you are generous with your time, talent, or treasure, the gift blesses both the giver and receiver!

God is ready to bless us when we are generous, and he has some guidelines for giving.

- *God expects us to invest in one another.* We bless the Lord when we are obedient to give, but he does not consider it heroic. It is evidence of a redeemed life, a grateful attitude. "Do not withhold good from those who deserve it when it's in your power to help them" (Proverbs 3:27 NLT). Who could be more deserving than the one who's pledged to spend life together with you?

- *A gift given out of obligation does not impress the Lord.* "So let each one *give* as he purposes in his heart, not grudgingly or of necessity; for God loves a cheerful giver" (2 Corinthians 9:7 NKJV). A gift given with a stingy attitude may meet a need, but God is looking at the heart. The attitude of *I have to* strips the joy of giving and may send your spouse the message *You owe me.* That's not generosity.

- *God's investment strategy is the most secure plan available.*
  "And God is able to bless you abundantly, so that in all
  things at all times, having all that you need, you will
  abound in every good work" (2 Corinthians 9:8 NIV).
  When you choose generosity, investing time, talent, and
  treasure in your spouse will produce a reliable return. It
  may come in many forms: gratitude, peace, increased closeness or intimacy—all good for building a healthy marriage.

God is the ultimate giver. He *chose* to send his Son, whose
life had such value it was sufficient to redeem the life of every
man, woman, and child who would ever live. Christ *chose* to
come, knowing how his life on earth would end. He gave it all
freely, no strings attached. He is our example of generosity.

Ron's generosity with me has been a hallmark of our life
together for nearly forty years. It comes naturally to him. I'm
grateful for his leadership; his example has inspired me to give
generously as well.

When it comes to generosity with your spouse, what will you
choose?

> *Conventional wisdom: "By what we get, we make a living.
> By what we give, we make a life."*
> —UNKNOWN

Chapter 14 Choice Questions:
I Choose to Be Generous with You

1. Time, talent, and treasure: How generous are you in these three areas? Which is easiest? Which is the hardest?
2. For each of the three areas, identify at least one act of generosity that would be meaningful to your spouse:
   - Time
   - Talent
   - Treasure
3. Where will you begin? What will you choose to do, starting today, to be generous with your mate?

Use the prayer below to declare your choice—or create one of your own.

Prayer: Heavenly Father, you are a generous God. Your gifts to us are beyond measure, and you have blessed us without hesitation. My desire is to follow your example and be generous with my husband/wife. I will actively seek opportunities to bless my spouse in gifts of time, talent, and treasure. I will not withhold what I can freely give. Show me circumstances where I can contribute, and I ask you to prompt me when I am slow to respond. I thank you for establishing and enriching our relationship to even greater depths as I choose to be generous.

I CHOOSE INTIMACY WITH YOU

I belong to my lover and my lover belongs to me.
—Song of Songs 6:3

I had dropped off the envelope with my husband's admin, picked up the babysitter, and packed an overnight bag. The anticipation of an entire night away was exciting. Ron was certain to be puzzled by my note, but I knew he'd enjoy what I had planned.

Carol, his assistant (and my partner in crime), stopped him as he headed out the door. "Oh, I nearly forgot. Deb dropped this off for you earlier today. She said it's important." She handed him the envelope and waved him out the door. "See you Monday. Have a great weekend!" Then she called me. "Elvis has left the building," she laughed.

"Thanks, Carol. Did he say anything?"

"No, he opened it on his way to the car though. I watched through the window. Then he stopped and looked around the parking lot like there might be something he'd missed. Hilarious. Have a great time, and enjoy one another." Carol was divorced and on her own. She missed that intimate connection of marriage.

Ron's note led him to our favorite restaurant. He checked the lot for my car. Not there. He went inside and took a quick look around. Nothing. Then the owner walked toward him with a carryout order—and another envelope. This one read:

Tonight is just for me and you; I hope you find me, yes, I do!

So think of oaks, or elms—just two, a spot for weary travelers who might find a place to lay their heads upon a giant feathery bed!

Two trees? A place for travelers to sleep? A smile began to spread across his face. The DoubleTree Hotel near the airport, just a few minutes from the restaurant.

When Ron arrived, he realized he had no idea which room I was in. When he asked at the desk, the clerk smiled and handed him yet one more envelope. This one contained a math problem, based on dates any husband should readily know. "She's really making me work for this," he said out loud. It took him a few minutes, and he had to call my mom to verify one item, but eventually he solved the equation and knew where he would find me.

In those days, three little boys made for a busy household. Wonderful, but busy. Moments on the couch late at night were often interrupted by a call—"Mama! I need a drink of water!"— or a sleepy toddler dragging a stuffed animal into the living room, flushed and feverish after a perfectly normal day. Time for intimacy got kicked in the teeth on a regular basis.

I'm not just talking *behind closed doors* intimacy. *One-on-one conversation* intimacy suffered too.

Intimacy is not optional in a healthy marriage. God created us with a strong need for connection, physically *and* emotionally. Genesis 2:24 reminds us we become *one flesh*. That's a little hard to maintain when you can't get five minutes alone together.

Physical and emotional satisfaction are codependent; sex without emotion was never God's plan. The world around us—movies, music, popular culture—suggests that the physical satisfaction of our sexuality, with no emotional connection or commitment, is all you really need. *Make the fireworks happen. The end.*

Baloney. That's two people using one another for personal gratification.

Don't misunderstand, the fireworks are great; God thought up the fireworks! Our sexuality is a gift from him designed to create pleasure. Proverbs 5:18-19 says: "Let your wife be a fountain of blessing for you. Rejoice in the wife of your youth. She is a loving deer, a graceful doe. Let her breasts satisfy you always. May you always be captivated by her love" (NLT). Sounds like pleasure to me.

Emotional intimacy is the result of sharing the foxhole when times get tough.

But couples end up in divorce court every week even as they tell their closest friends, "The sex was great, but it wasn't enough."

Strong emotional connection in marriage without physical fulfillment creates frustration and leaves the relationship at risk. God warns us of the potential consequences in 1 Corinthians 7:5: "Do not deprive each other of sexual relations, unless you both agree to refrain from sexual intimacy so you can give yourselves more completely to prayer. Afterward you should come together again so that Satan won't be able to tempt you because of your lack of self-control" (NLT).

Intimacy, true intimacy, requires connecting mind *and* body, the physical and emotional. That's the whole package—and a secret not just to making love, but to making your love last.

One of the challenges is that men and women don't always have the same view of intimacy. For example, the woman's view might include:

- Holding hands over a special dinner followed by a walk on a moonlit beach. Deep conversation about the couple's goals and hopes for the relationship, both openly sharing their hearts while cuddling by a fire as the waves crest nearby. When they arrive home, she's feeling connected and ready for some closed-door time with her hubby.

Her husband's view:

- Dinner's good. A walk is fine. "Aren't you about ready to head home? It's getting late and I don't want to be too tired by the time we get home, now that we finally have the house to ourselves. We can talk in the car on the way if you want to tell me about stuff."

I admit it's a little stereotypical. Women are often ready to cut to the chase, and men really enjoy a moonlit walk on the beach once in a while. *That's the point.* We need to understand and honor each other's needs to make it work.

Emotional intimacy is the result of sharing the foxhole when times get tough. Disclosing your greatest hopes and your darkest fears to one another. Taking in the movie your spouse wants to see while holding hands in the dark. And if you need more ideas, review the chapters in this book on generosity, romance, pursuit, and forgiveness.

A few tips to get your wheels turning on how to begin:

- E-mail one another throughout the day; flirt or let your spouse know you've been thinking about him or her.
- Read the book of the Song of Solomon out loud together. Look for examples in the dialogue of both emotional and physical connections.
- Carve out time to have important discussions about matters of the heart. Let your spouse in on your thoughts and concerns.
- Lovingly teach your spouse how to demonstrate love for you, meeting both your physical and emotional needs. Ask your mate to do the same.
- Burn the candles, use the nice sheets, and splash the perfume. Don't save it for a special occasion; today is special.
- Get a babysitter; get away; get a room.

As long as I live, I'll never forget the look in Ron's eyes when I opened that hotel room door. I won't let you in on all the intimate details of the next twenty-four hours, but let's just say it was a night to remember.

Mind and body. Emotional and physical. Put them together and you have a winning combination of intimacy. What will you choose today?

Conventional wisdom: "If I had my life to live over, I'd have fewer meetings and more rendezvous."
—ROBERT BRAULT

Chapter 15 Choice Questions:
I Choose Intimacy with You

1. Complete these statements:
   - I currently meet my spouse's emotional needs by:
   - I currently meet my spouse's physical needs by:
2. Respond to this:
   - I've never told my spouse how I feel about our level of intimacy, and it would help him/her to know...
3. Where will you start? What will you choose to do, starting today, to meet your mate's physical and emotional needs? Use the information from items 2 and 3 above to create your plan.

Use the prayer below to declare your choice—or create one of your own.

Prayer: Lord, you created us to be complementary beings—uniquely different but each completing the other. When our emotional and physical needs are met, there is unity and satisfaction in our life together. I choose to protect and promote our marriage by meeting these needs for my husband/wife. I believe as I endeavor to take care of my spouse's needs, my needs will be met as well. I ask that you help me express my needs and ask my mate to help me understand his/her needs as well. I choose intimacy with my spouse.

CHAPTER 16

I CHOOSE TO KEEP ROMANCE ALIVE

Kiss me and kiss me again, for your love is sweeter than wine.

—Song of Songs 1:2 (NLT)

I t was the end of a very long day. My colleagues and I had presented an eight-hour training session for a group of industry leaders. When we finished our presentation, we packed up our supplies and drove three hours to a new city in order to do it all again the following day. We had located our hotel training room and started to unpack supplies and ready the room for the group who'd arrive in the morning. All five of us were about out of gas, tired to the bone.

"I'm looking for the birthday girl. Which one of you is Jane?" The uniformed staff member glanced at the group of weary women.

"I'm Jane. And how did you know it was my birthday?"

"I have a delivery for you," he said as he headed off down the hall. Moments later, he wheeled in a cart laden with beautiful chocolate-covered strawberries, cheese and crackers, and assorted nuts. A bottle of something fizzy graced the presentation. A white envelope lay on the cart. She opened it, and a smile quickly appeared.

"Oh that Jimmy!" she laughed as she read the card. Her husband, on the other side of the country this night, had been unwilling to let her special day pass unheralded. His birthday wish requested that she enjoy the special spread with her friends and colleagues.

We all *oohed* and *aahed* over his romantic surprise. "Wow, Jane! What a guy," someone said. We all nodded.

"He's a keeper, Janie. Hang on to that one."

Jimmy's gesture inspired us all, and suddenly, a new level of energy swept the group. We dove into the goodies and chatted about "what a wonderful guy Jimmy is." And not one of us had ever met him.

And the romance didn't stop there. When Jane arrived home late the next night, the house was dark and Jimmy was asleep. Jane noticed a light on in the dining room. There she found flowers and two tickets to Italy laid out on the table with another *Happy Birthday* wish. That Jimmy. What a show-off!

Jim and Jane are blessed with a loving marriage that's still filled with tenderness and affection after many years; you can see it in Jane's eyes when she talks about him. They show up for one another, and they show off their love for one another. They're keeping romance alive.

Some of us (most of us) aren't planning romantic trips to Italy and celebrating with chocolate-covered strawberries—a sink full of dirty dishes, an overflowing clothes hamper, and a teething toddler can put that dream to bed quickly. But it doesn't mean we can't keep romance on the front burner.

"Sex starts in the kitchen," my husband announced after attending a men's event.

"Really? Well, there's not even a cleared-off counter for that kind of horseplay in here," I replied as I wiped a sticky spill from the floor.

He explained, "The speaker today reminded us that what happens when the lights go down is tied to the

Romance reminds your spouse why he or she fell in love with you in the first place. And who couldn't use a little memory jogger when life is piling up on you?

day's interactions, so today, you go read a book or take a long bath. I'll feed the boys lunch and take them to the park. Forget about cooking this evening; let's order pizza."

Trust me—that was as grand a gesture in the romance department as I could imagine. At that particular point in my life, it was way better than chocolate-covered strawberries!

The *Merriam-Webster Dictionary* defines romance as:

- to try to influence or curry favor with, especially by lavishing personal attention, gifts, or flattery.
- to carry on a love affair with.
- and my personal addition: to court or woo.

But just as the things that romance us, or that draw us to another, may change or expand over time, so does the definition of romance.

Real romance doesn't have to include lavish gifts or extravagance, although it may. Extravagant can be a European vacation or a weekend away at a bed-and-breakfast—it's relative to your situation. Sometimes a simple movie date and dinner are a luxury, especially if it's a surprise. It communicates a desire to get away, just the two of you.

Romance isn't a one-size-fits-all look that remains the same season after season. It keeps the individual in mind—as my keenly observant husband had figured out. It's intentional; specific to the one you are courting. Don't take me to see the Cowboys play in Dallas. Tickets to a James Taylor concert are more likely to melt my heart. This says, "I thought about *you* when I picked this out."

Men need to be romanced as much as women do. It makes them know they're needed and desired. A husband rarely expects his wife to flirt with him, but when she does, it can create a sweet spark of tenderness and connection.

Romance is about making the person you love feel special, and there are dozens of ways to do it. Load the dishwasher for her, wash his car, or suggest a walk. Put a note in his briefcase or in her lunch, or a sticky note on his steering wheel. I once stunned my husband by mowing the lawn. (Note it says *once*.) Make a sandwich, make a date, make a baby!

Romance reminds your spouse why he or she fell in love with you in the first place. And who couldn't use a little memory jogger when life is piling up on you? So today, what about a little romance? What will you choose to keep romance alive?

Conventional wisdom: "Once in a while, right in the middle of an ordinary life, love gives us fairy tales."
—Unknown

Chapter 16 Choice Questions:
I Choose to Keep Romance Alive

1. How are you doing when it comes to keeping romance alive? On a scale of 1 to 5, with 5 being a significant and consistent effort, where do you land? What do you do (or not do) that earns you that score?
2. What would romance your spouse? What could you say or do to communicate, "I'm thinking about you today," and make him/her feel special? List at least three ideas.
3. Life can get in the way of romance. Often we're tired or busy. What can you do to make sure you keep romance on the front burner? What will you do today to romance your husband/wife?

Use the prayer below to declare your choice—or create one of your own.

Prayer: You romance your church, Lord, your bride. We are always on your mind. It keeps us connected and close, secure in your love for us. I desire for my spouse to know that same security and connectedness in our marriage. Each and every day I want to make known, "I'm thinking of you today." My husband/wife deserves my attention and needs my intentional and thoughtful expression of love. I'm committed to ensuring he/she receives it. I pray you will grow my awareness, Lord, of specific ways to romance my mate. Please draw my attention to those things that would impress my love on his/her heart. Today, I choose to keep romance alive!

CHAPTER 17

I CHOOSE TO STAND IN AGREEMENT WITH YOU

Can two walk together, unless they are agreed?
—Amos 3:3 (NKJV)

I could tell by the way he walked up the driveway. Something was wrong. Terribly wrong.

"Hey, babe. How was your day?"

"Not good," Ron said. He looked as forlorn as I'd ever seen him.

We were preparing to leave within the hour for our youngest son's high school graduation. But I knew this couldn't wait. "What's wrong?"

"I got laid off today. They eliminated my position."

Those words should have set off a warning light in my brain, but instead, an alarm bell rang in my heart. "Hallelujah! This is how it starts!" He looked at me as though I'd lost my mind.

But I hadn't. For several years we'd been standing together in agreement, praying, trusting, and working toward a dream God had planted in our hearts: full-time ministry for Ron.

Two years earlier, through prayer, God had given us a clear plan—a path with several important components for preparation:

- Ron was to return to Bible school.
- We were to spend a year in prayer and study together.
- We were to clear any and all debt.

It was both exciting and overwhelming. Although it was beyond anything we imagined, we were in absolute agreement: God directed this plan. We shared it with very few people, not wanting a cross-examination of how it would ever be possible. We weren't sure how it would happen, but we were clear. It *would* happen.

When looking at the three items on that list, how could we not have questions? We both worked full-time, had one son in high school and another living at home. The third son attended a private college. We squeaked by to pay his tuition each month. We lived in an area with a tremendously high cost of living. Get out of debt? Dedicate a year to prayer and study? Bible school? We couldn't even begin to figure it out.

But God. That became our phrase. So for two years, we prayed. We dreamed. We saved a few dollars here and there. Our agreement didn't falter. And when that alarm bell rang, I recognized it clearly. "Don't you think the timing's interesting? The last day of high school for our youngest is the day you get laid off? Don't look for a job. Go to school!" With my reputation as a recovering worrier, this was not the reaction Ron expected.

He wasn't immediately convinced. He worried about the finances and putting pressure on me. How would people react if he didn't look for a job? And how could we pay for Bible school and get completely out of debt with one less income? We had made small progress in the previous two years, but this seemed insurmountable. "Do you think I can do this? Are we ready for it?" he asked.

"I believe in what God asked us to do. We're ready."

Ron agreed to take the summer off, spending it in prayer and study, and deferring a decision until the fall. But I knew he'd begun to find peace.

As the leaves turned, he made his decision—he would return to school. Times were not easy. On occasion we grew concerned about finances, especially tuition for two in school. We stood together in prayer, united, agreed. Each time, God was faithful. We learned an important lesson: what God orders, he pays for.

We need to trust the Lord, be patient and stand unified in our agreement. When we do our part, God does his.

Late that year, when I suggested we consider a move to Texas, God smiled. It hadn't been my idea at all. We sold our home in three days, with several bids *over* the asking price. We hadn't realized the high cost of living in our area meant our house would sell for more than two-and-a-half times what we'd paid for it only eight years earlier! We eliminated all debt and bought a new home with cash in a single move. God's checklist for us was complete. Never on our own could we have figured out the plan

God had in place. We needed to trust him, be patient, and stand unified in our agreement. When we did our part, God did his.

Texas has been a wonderful home for us. We found wonderful friends who share our faith and have become family. God has blessed our willingness to follow his plan, his way.

Ron has been all over the world teaching and ministering in the nine years since our move. He's led retreats for hundreds of men in India, Russia, Uganda, and Zimbabwe. He's heading soon to Guatemala. And he's also involved in getting clean water and shoes to children in nations where there is desperate need.

Life is often a puzzle. We can see part of the picture, but it's not always clear what it will look like when all is complete. It's tempting to get anxious and attempt to fill in the empty spots on our own. Yet Ron and I wouldn't have been able to agree together on all God designed for us had we been given every puzzle piece at once. He delivered the pieces one at a time, as we were able to manage, knowing our faith would grow bit by bit as the picture was revealed. What a glorious and merciful Father he is!

Conventional wisdom: "*Sometimes I've believed six impossible things before breakfast!*"
—Lewis Carroll

Chapter 17 Choice Questions:
I Choose to Stand in Agreement with You

1. There is power in agreement; without it, two cannot walk in the same direction. In which areas of life do you and your spouse walk in agreement? Where do you lack agreement? Finances? Child rearing? Time management, choice of friends, or extracurricular activities? Other?

2. What steps have you attempted to close the gap between you? What is the lack of agreement costing you?

3. What does God's Word say about the area in which you struggle? Discuss your concerns (without judgment or anger) with your spouse. What are you willing to do today to walk in agreement?

Use the prayer below to declare your choice—or create one of your own.

Prayer: Father, I know there is power in agreement; your Word is clear: "If two of you *agree* here on earth concerning anything you ask, my Father in heaven will do it for you." Without agreement, our prayers are hindered. My heart's desire is to walk in unity with my spouse and with your Word. Where we are in agreement, I thank you and ask you to help us stand together, resisting fear regardless of circumstances. Where we lack agreement, I pray you will clearly show us your will. Help us to submit to one another as we submit to you. My desire is to walk together in the singular, focused direction you have designed for us as husband and wife.

I CHOOSE
TO CHALLENGE YOU

As iron sharpens iron, so a friend sharpens a friend.
—Proverbs 27:17 (NLT)

I am not okay with this. You've been suspicious for some time. And now David's all but confirmed he's been having an affair with the admin in your department." Rachel looked across the table at her husband.

"I shouldn't have said anything to you," he answered. "David's my friend. I don't really want to get involved in all of this. It's none of my business."

"You're right, it's not. But you can't pretend you don't know what you know, Zack." Rachel was frustrated with her husband's attitude. "Marcy is our friend too. We see them at church, and the kids have playdates every week. What are we supposed to do? Smile as though nothing's wrong?"

"This is not ours to sort out, Rachel. David's the one who has to make this right." Zack ran his hands through his hair. "C'mon, let's not make their problem our problem, okay?"

"I don't believe you can say that. He's a church elder. You were his best man at their wedding. You have a responsibility to him *and* to her. He obviously needs you to remind him of his vows." Rachel went on, "If the situation was reversed and David knew I was seeing someone, wouldn't you expect him to address it *because* he's your friend?"

Zack was quiet for a moment. "Yeah, I suppose I would. I just don't know what to say to him. It's so awkward. David's campaigning to put Stephanie into the marketing role, even though she's not qualified. He's always got some excuse as to why he can't go to lunch with the team, but then he and Steph slip out of the office together." Zack pressed his lips tightly in a grim line. "But this morning clinched it. I saw them at the coffee shop— they were sitting real close, whispering and laughing. They never even noticed I was there." Zack looked away. "When I told him I had seen them at coffee, his face said everything I needed to know. Later I caught up with him in the parking lot and asked him point-blank if he was having an affair with Stephanie. He didn't answer me. Said to stay out of it and walked off."

As members of Christ's body, we are to hold one another accountable for how we live and to encourage righteous living in one another.

Rachel reached out to cover her husband's hand. "I know how tough that must have been. You guys have been friends since college. I'm sorry you're in this position. What are you going to do? It's not okay to help him cheat on Marcy by remaining quiet."

"So that's how you see it, Rachel? If I choose to stay out of it, I'm helping him?"

Rachel nodded.

"What am I supposed to do?" Zack asked. "Tell his wife that he's cheating? Maybe it's just some flirting. Maybe nothing has really happened."

Rachel looked carefully at her husband. "Then maybe you have a chance to make sure nothing more *does* happen."

Zack felt miserable, but he knew his wife was right. He also knew he would need help figuring out what to do next. His friendship with David was important to him.

Our life in Christ comes with responsibilities and obligations to one another. As members of his body, we are to hold one another accountable for how we live and to encourage righteous living in one another: "And let us consider *and* give attentive, continuous care to watching over one another, studying how we may stir up (stimulate and incite) to love *and* helpful deeds and noble activities" (Hebrews 10:24 AMP).

Rachel is living this scripture as she attempts to influence Zack to address the situation. If Zack decides to speak with his friend, he too is *stirring up and inciting David to noble activities*. Or at least to facing the music.

Husbands and wives have the opportunity to help one another develop spiritually by challenging thoughts, actions, and decisions that are not in line with God's Word. But this can be tricky territory. Those closest to us may know our intentions are good and, as a result, give us a pass on taking the necessary action. God expects couples to influence each other in a productive manner that leads to an outcome influenced by his Spirit. We can accomplish this in several ways.

- We can model Christ in our daily lives. Actions often speak louder than words.
- We can provide personal insight to help make the situation clearer.
- We can share scriptures to help identify the role God would ask us to accept in a difficult circumstance.
- We can pray for and with our spouse for wisdom and direction on how to approach the situation.
- We can demonstrate that we too are open to spiritual growth and maturity by welcoming our spouses to challenge our thoughts and actions.
- We can accept correction with humility.

To confront the issue without getting confrontational helps lead to a positive and peaceable conclusion. When iron sharpens iron, sparks may fly, so taking the steps to build a firewall is a good idea.

Remember that loving someone doesn't mean you will always agree with everything they say or do. A loving spouse who challenges you to become mature in the Lord, helping you to examine your thoughts and actions to conform to the image of Christ, is a gift indeed.

Zack and Rachel prayed together and talked through the night. Zack has a plan for tomorrow: He will speak to David and let him know he must tell Marcy the truth and resign from his position at church. Zack will also tell him if he fails to do so in the next two days, Zack will have no other option but to tell

Marcy, as well as their pastor. He's nervous about the conversation, but confident it's the right decision.

Zack and Rachel are praying it doesn't come to this, but they are willing to stand together to do what is right. They've navigated a difficult situation, growing stronger and more mature as a couple in the process.

Let the sparks fly.

> *Conventional wisdom: "It's nice to be around people who think differently than you. They challenge your ideas and keep you from being complacent."*
> —TUCKER CARLSON

Chapter 18 Choice Questions:
I Choose to Challenge You

1. What's your typical reaction when you are challenged by your spouse? How does your spouse respond to being challenged by you?
2. What's your typical approach to challenging your spouse? Is it based on your experience, your preference, or on scriptural principles? How might your approach influence the way your spouse responds?
3. What steps can you use to challenge your spouse in order to influence him/her to greater maturity and growth in the Lord? What will you choose to do?

Use the prayer below to declare your choice—or create one of your own.

Prayer: Lord, I desire to grow daily and to become more like you. I choose to be open to my spouse when he/she challenges my thoughts or actions and provides a scripture or spiritual principle to correct my course. I pray you will give me courage when I feel prompted by your Spirit to address my spouse, and I ask that you allow me to approach the discussion in a way that confronts the behavior without becoming confrontational. Please give me the words that will communicate my best intention for my husband/wife without creating unnecessary offense or hurt. My desire is that we grow spiritually strong as a couple. I choose to accept my role in accomplishing that goal.

CHAPTER 19

I CHOOSE TO BE OPEN
AND HONEST WITH YOU

Instead, by speaking the truth with love, let's grow in every
way into Christ.
—EPHESIANS 4:15

Brett returned home from work to find Marni quiet. Too
quiet.

They had arrived home late last night after dinner with
a group of friends. Brett had thoroughly enjoyed their time
together, and Marni seemed to enjoy it as well. She had been
silent on the ride home, but it was nearly midnight, and Brett
thought little of it. They both had an early start at work this
morning and each had hurried to get out of the house on time.
There was little opportunity for conversation, and again, he
hadn't considered that something might be wrong.

Until now.

She had barely looked up when he walked in the door, and
she seemed preoccupied with the mail in her lap.

"What's wrong, babe?" he asked.

"Nothing." Marni looked at the floor while twisting a piece of her hair.

"You seem very quiet."

She shrugged, stood, and headed for the kitchen. And the silence continued.

Sound familiar?

We may share a last name with our spouses, but we don't share a brain. How will Brett know that a remark he made last night embarrassed and hurt her? *He won't.* How will he be able to prevent it from happening again? *He can't.* How will he and Marni get back on the same page and move beyond the silence? *Not possible.*

Is your spouse in the dark about your negative feelings?

Remember the enemy does his best work in darkness. But when light appears, darkness must flee.

Not possible *unless* Marni is willing to be open and honest about what happened and how it made her feel.

Openness and honesty are choices: Will we *submit* our thoughts, our feelings, and our concerns to our spouses? The dictionary includes several definitions for the word *submit*, including this one: "to present to another for review or consideration." Would you like your thoughts, your hurts, your feelings considered? Submit them, present them, to allow your spouse to understand you more fully and make different choices in the future.

For many people, the discomfort that comes with such a level of transparency is overwhelming. This isn't uncommon. Often when we experience hurt or disappointment, we pull into ourselves and away from others. Sometimes it's done to avoid conflict. Sometimes it might seem trivial. Too many times, the silence can be a test.

If he really loves me, he will ask what's on my mind.

I'm going to wait to see how long it takes her to notice I'm upset.

Instead, ask yourself: *Am I testing my spouse? Am I keeping score? What thoughts or feelings am I keeping to myself that the enemy could use to divide my spouse and me?*

It might not even be something that happened between the two of you. Old wounds from other relationships can run deep, and they surface when we are vulnerable or have not dealt openly with them. Are you holding fear, worry, hurt, concern, or issues in secret? Is your spouse in the dark about them? Remember that the enemy does his best work in darkness. But when light appears, darkness must flee.

Secrets hold us hostage to our feelings, and the *strength* of the secret is *silence*.

Usually, there are some visible signs beyond silence that all is not well: withdrawal, impatience, quickness to anger or to show frustration. Your spouse experiences the symptoms but may be clueless as to the cause. We can't fix what we don't realize is broken.

The guessing game may continue on Brett's part. He may bring home flowers tomorrow or offer to clean up the kitchen, all in an effort to fix whatever is broken.

Or he may join Marni in her silence.

We can do this better by making a choice. Today.

> *Conventional Wisdom: "The best person to talk with about the problems in your relationship is the person you're in a relationship with."*
>
> —UNKNOWN

Chapter 19 Choice Questions:
I Choose to Be Open and Honest with You

1. Which feelings or thoughts are difficult for you to express (submit) to your spouse? Why?
2. What do you experience when you choose to keep your thoughts or feelings hidden? What's it costing you? What's it costing your spouse?
3. What does your spouse experience when you withhold your thoughts and feelings? What are the signs?
4. How will you push past your hesitance to be open and honest? What conversation do you need to have with your spouse to help him/her know how to help you? What will you choose today?

Use the prayer below to declare your choice—or create one of your own.

Prayer: Father, I choose to show my reverence for your Son by submitting to my husband/wife, openly sharing my heart and mind. I believe that marriage is most successful, and you are honored, when we submit to your plan: the two shall become one, united in you. I will choose today to be upfront with him/her, submitting my thoughts and feelings so they may be considered, refusing to let silence send the message or to test my spouse's commitment to our marriage or to me. I will not wait until asked, but will choose to offer my hurts, my ideas, and my concerns to my mate. I know you provide the strength and courage to accomplish what you ask of us. I trust you will use my transparency to strengthen our marriage and our life together in you.

CHAPTER 20

I CHOOSE TO LISTEN TO YOU

You hear with your ears, but you don't really listen.
—Isaiah 42:20 (NLT)

What did you say? Jake...I can't hear you...I love you. Are you there?"

The connection was terrible—again. The constant hum of static punctuated by the occasional loud pop had become so frustrating. Hearing Jake's voice was nearly impossible.

Cori pressed her cell phone tighter against her head, straining to hear, hot tears threatening to spill over. The few calls Jake could make from his overseas duty station were precious, but she was often upset when they concluded. Hearing only every other word made communication difficult, but she lived for each phrase she could make out and prayed each day for the phone to ring. She hadn't known how precious these calls, simply a few stolen bits of conversation, would become.

When was the last time your spouse listened to you with that level of intensity? When was the last time you offered it to your spouse?

Being heard is one of our greatest human needs. It connects us to others and helps them understand who we are. Knowing we are understood is essential to intimacy in relationships. It's hard to be transparent with others, even your spouse, if you believe they just don't *get* you.

Being *heard* and being *understood* are linked—both are needed to see the whole picture, just as a lock needs a key to open a door.

Listening creates connections at an intimate level. But few of us are good listeners; most of us have a preference for talking instead. How often do you hear someone say, "Boy, if I just had a good talker in my life…"? Typically our dance card is full of good talkers. Good listeners are harder to come by.

Listening is never accidental; it's always on purpose. The listener is invested in the life of the talker.

One of the questions I will ask God when I have the chance is this: When I talked to my husband and he looked directly at me, smiling, nodding, and saying "uh-huh" at all the right times, but was *absolutely not* listening to me, why couldn't you have placed a small red light in the middle of his forehead that flashed the words, *Save your breath*?

I know listening is not the ultimate indicator of Ron's love for me. But after Jesus, he's the most important person in my life. I want to share my *stuff* with him: experiences, thoughts, ideas, and concerns. I know he cares, so why isn't he more attentive?

And honestly, I'm not any better (and perhaps not as good) at giving him my undivided attention. We can both do this better.

It's not as though we set out deliberately *not* to listen, fingers plugging our ears while saying, "*La la la la*—I can't hear you!" Listening is difficult to do. We *hear* with our ears. But we *listen* with the heart and mind—big difference.

Listening only happens as a matter of choice.

We might overhear a conversation not intended for us or pick up background noise while reading. But that's *ear* activity. Heart-and-mind activity requires much more. Listening is never accidental; it's always on purpose. The listener is invested in the life of the talker.

Sometimes our inability or unwillingness to set aside our own stuff in the moment prevents us from listening at the level required for genuine understanding. Husbands and wives often struggle with this. You burst through the door, purse under your chin, mail between your teeth, grocery bags hanging from both arms. He greets you, takes the mail, and immediately launches into animated conversation about an opportunity at work. Big promotion possible, more money—isn't it exciting? You just want to collapse, but you have groceries to put away, a dinner to prepare, and kids demanding attention.

Then you realize he's stopped talking and looks: (a) wounded, (b) angry, (c) confused. Maybe all three. Would you like to hear more? Yes, but not *now*. Maybe you've had a tough day at work or you're not feeling well. Some sort of life-stuff makes this a bad time for such an important discussion. You simply can't—you don't have the *ability* to do it right now.

On the other hand, you may be swept up by a great movie on TV. Perhaps you're finishing a terrific book or headed out the door to garden, and the request comes: "Got a minute?" You have a choice to make. Do you break away and prefer your spouse? Do you promise time after you've finished without even knowing the importance of the request? Sometimes we are *unwilling* to make time to listen. It's always a choice.

What is required to be a really good listener? How can we become better listeners?

- When your spouse needs to talk, ask yourself: *Is now the right time?* If you can't do it at the moment, share the reason for the delay and identify why it will be more beneficial to wait.

- Rather than saying, "Now's not a good time," identify *when* you can be fully available. Perhaps after the kids are in bed, or once you've finished prepping for tomorrow's presentation.

- If now *is* the right time, find a quiet place and minimize distractions. Turn off the TV and silence the cell phone. This communicates, "You have my full attention."

- Come to the table with an open heart and open mind. Set aside your need to interject your own thoughts before your spouse has fully expressed his or her thoughts..

- Ask questions to gain *complete* understanding—the whole picture—but do not interrupt.

You have a choice. Make it a good one.

Conventional wisdom: The first duty of love is to listen.
—Paul Tillich

Chapter 20 Choice Questions:
I Choose to Listen to You

1. What challenges do you face that make listening difficult for you? What distracts you when listening to your spouse?
2. Read back in this chapter for examples of the inability to listen. What has your spouse tried to discuss with you that you have been *unable* to fully listen to? How can you make yourself more available?
3. What topics have you been *unwilling* to discuss or listen to from your spouse? Why? What will you do today to choose a willing, hearing heart?

Use the prayer below to declare your choice—or create one of your own.

Prayer: Father, you used the word *listen* so often when speaking to your children, almost as though we had to be reminded to focus—even on *your* words. I ask you, Lord, to remind me through the voice of your Holy Spirit to listen with both heart and mind to my spouse. I surrender my time and my will to intentionally listen for the purpose of deeper understanding and transparency as a couple. I pray that our ability and willingness to live with open hearts and minds leads us to greater intimacy in our relationship. Today, Lord, I choose to listen.

I CHOOSE TO LAUGH
WITH YOU

*A joyful heart helps healing, but a broken spirit dries up the
bones.*

—PROVERBS 17:22

What was *that* all about?" I stood reeling from the frontal
assault, hands on my hips, glaring at Ron. He wore a
mischievous smirk that annoyed me intensely.

"It's a pillow fight! It's fun!" He hoisted another pillow in the
air and prepared to let it fly.

"It's not fun. Don't do that again." I stalked off in a huff, leaving my newlywed husband to finish making the bed.

I like fun as much as the next person. That was not fun. But
my husband will tell you that my upbringing—without siblings
my age to share daily life with—left me a little on the stuffy side
when it comes to fun like pillow fights or wrestling or pouring a
glass of ice water on someone in a hot shower. You get the point.

As a mom of three sons, I discovered there was a world of so-called humor I knew nothing of. Much of it involved things I found repulsive, which made the boys laugh even harder. Grossing out Mom was a favorite pastime, and I have to admit, some of it did make me laugh.

I *love* to laugh, and so does my husband. We discovered early in our marriage that if we could laugh about it, we could get through it. It wasn't funny *in the moment* when I nearly crushed him by starting a car while he worked beneath it. But once we knew he was okay, it was pretty darn funny. He could have been angry; instead, we laughed.

Laughter under wraps is one of the best experiences you'll ever have. You know, those times when it's not appropriate to laugh but you can't stop yourself. Ron and I once boarded a five-hour midnight flight to Hawaii. Most of our fellow passengers pulled out pillows and eyeshades in the darkened cabin, planning to snooze their way to the tropics. But my husband wasn't tired. He leafed through the airline entertainment magazine and discovered several of his favorite comedians could be found on the in-flight system. He plugged in his earphones and settled in to hear Bill Cosby, Bob Newhart, and Foster Brooks.

Laughter connects us in ways that few other experiences do. If we can laugh about it, we can get through it.

It started with a few chuckles. Then a hearty laugh. I poked him. "*Shh!* People are trying to sleep." He nodded, but moments later the giggles began to overtake him. Now people were giving him dirty looks, and I was getting caught in the crossfire. I murmured an apology and shook my head disapprovingly, hoping they hadn't realized we were together. No such luck.

He quieted briefly and I closed my eyes. Within moments, an eruption of laughter pierced the quiet, followed by gasping for air. He pulled off the earphones in a desperate attempt to contain the hysteria when the unthinkable happened. I began to laugh.

I wasn't laughing at the comedy program; I wasn't listening to it. Something about his attempt to stifle his unbridled joy struck me as funny. Ron and I laughed until we cried. Each time one of us would pull it together, the other would totally lose control. We couldn't even look at each other for at least twenty minutes.

Let's just say we didn't make any friends on that flight.

Laughter connects us to others in ways that few other experiences do. Think about the last time you saw a funny movie with someone. Research says when there's a great comedic line, we look at one another when we laugh. Why? My guess is that laughter shared is the very best kind. Together we find it funny, and we want to connect over our joint amusement.

You don't need to be a master joke teller to share humor with your honey—the day's observations and experiences can make for great fun. We once watched a little girl at the beach, sitting on her daddy's lap eating the biggest snow cone we'd ever seen. She began digging into the side of the ice with a small spoon, tunneling her way to the other side. "Watch this," Ron said as he bumped my arm and nodded in their direction. "This is gonna be good." Within moments, that bright red icy snowball came crashing down the front of her daddy's bare chest so fast that he nearly dumped her on the sand when he jumped to his feet. We could have called the impending disaster to the dad's attention, but where's the fun in that?

Here are a few tips for bringing laughter—and the connection it creates—into your life.

- *Go to funny movies or attend live comedy events together.* Clean comedy is available; search it out. Our son and his wife took us to see a favorite comedian as a Christmas gift. It was a great event, and sharing it with them gave us a year's worth of inside jokes to enjoy.

- *Send funny stories, anecdotes, or online videos to one another.* The Internet is full of funny moments. Everyone's got a video camera and can't resist posting their silly stuff.

- *Find your own silly spots.* The Hallmark store—an unlikely place—has cracked us up more than once. We've been found doubled over together in the birthday section while searching for just the right card. Bring your spouse along for a joint journey to humor land when somebody hands you the tickets.

- *Enjoy the* ha-has *and the* ahas. Did you ever notice that humorous moments often come with a lesson? (No more midnight flights!) Be sure to let your spouse in on the insights you stumble upon.

- *Choose joy during times of difficulty or hardship.* Each day, both good and bad, presents the chance to choose. When you find yourselves under tough circumstances, ask: "What am I doing down here?" Don't allow your feelings to dictate your level of joy. As believers, our joy is not in things but in knowing Jesus. Reflect on the goodness and examine God's track record in your life. As a couple, look at pictures or home movies to remind yourself of the joy God has given you.

- *Remember to laugh with one another, not at one another.* Use humor as a tool, not a weapon. Making someone the object of the joke can backfire, especially with an audience. Mean-spirited is not funny.

Life is serious business; there's not a punch line at the end of every story. But the very best medicine can be found, according to the Bible, in a heart determined to make merry in the midst of it all.

Choose to see the lighter side. Find the funny, even if you have to hunt it down. It's worth it.

> *Conventional wisdom: "A smile is the shortest distance between two people."*
> —VICTOR BORGE

Chapter 21 Choice Questions:
I Choose to Laugh with You

1. What do you and your spouse do for fun? What makes you laugh?
2. What can you do to ensure that laughter and joy are a regular part of your relationship? Identify at least three activities or steps you can take.
3. When challenge and hardship come, how will you choose to "take your medicine"? What can you do to choose joy and laughter during difficult times?

Use the prayer below to declare your choice—or create one of your own.

Prayer: Laughter is the best medicine, Lord. It connects us to one another and is an acknowledgment of the joy that comes in knowing you. Remind us daily to share the funny moments we encounter while we're apart. Inspire us to laugh at the little things so they don't become big things. Holy Spirit, lead me to seek joy in times of difficulty, and prompt me to bring cheer to my spouse when he or she is feeling down. I will actively seek ways to bring fun and laughter into our relationship. I thank you for this gift.

I CHOOSE TO ACKNOWLEDGE YOU

*Thank you for making me so wonderfully complex! Your
workmanship is marvelous—how well I know it.*
—Psalm 139:14 (NLT)

I t was one of those legendary California afternoons—sunny
with incredible azure-blue skies above. Ron tightly held my
hand as we walked across the high school tennis courts on our
way to my house. He had waited outside my last class to walk
me home, as he did every day. Once there, we'd linger on the
front porch for a few minutes, enjoying some time alone. At
seventeen, I thought this was about as good as it could get. We'd
been dating for several months, and it was clear—this guy was
a keeper.

"Do you know what first drew me to you, Deb? Any idea what
sparked my interest, that first attraction?" He shot me a sideways
look and smiled.

I didn't have a clue. *Maybe it was my smile or my eyes. People have often commented on my big brown eyes.* "No, Ron, I really don't. Never thought about it."

He stopped walking and faced me. His expression was suddenly serious. "You were interested in what I was thinking, in what was on my mind. You wanted to understand my thoughts and hear what I had to say." And with that, he turned and we resumed our stroll.

Huh. That's weird, is what I remember thinking at the time. But as our relationship developed, it made sense.

Ron grew up in a blended family. Three older stepbrothers were part of the bargain when his mom remarried, bringing the total number of siblings to six. It was a difficult mix that never really came together well. His two sisters shared a room, and Ron bunked with the rest of the boys. To say his brothers were troubled would be an understatement, and his stepdad was not an easy man to live with in those days. *Balanced on pins and needles* was a good description of daily life in his home.

One of the unspoken rules in the house was a simple but important guideline: *if you have an opinion, best keep it to yourself.* Mealtimes were for eating, not conversing. Staying off the radar was a daily endeavor.

So Ron had lots of thoughts packed down tightly, pushed aside to prevent them from spilling out. It broke my heart then, and it hurts now, to realize that something I took for granted had not been available to him: the chance to share thoughts, experiences, and opinions with those around us. And until I asked, it never dawned on him that *anyone* might ever be interested.

I *acknowledged* Ron on that walk home. And I don't mean that I was grateful or thankful for some act of kindness he had performed. The word *acknowledge* has several meanings. It can be used to express recognition or realization, as in: *I acknowledge the gifts and talents God placed in you.* It also means "to take notice of." To translate fully: I had recognized Ron as one who is valid. I took notice of who God called him to be.

That leisurely walk home after school was a turning point in Ron's young life, and in our life together. Until the age of seventeen, Ron had been pigeonholed—cornered by his circumstances and his experience. Without acknowledgment in his life, those experiences limited what he dreamed and believed his life could be.

Our life experiences leave marks. Some good. Some not so good. Those *experiences* form what we *believe* about ourselves and life in general. Those beliefs dictate our *actions*, and our actions define who we become. Good experiences lift us. Negative experiences hold us down.

But there's positive news. While we can't change people's past experiences, we can help create new ones for them that have the power to change their destiny. What I really did for Ron was build new experiences that revealed my high regard for him. I *acknowledged* his life; I appraised his worth at a far greater value than he had ever known or expected; I saw him as God does.

One who is acknowledged, able to walk in the fullness of who God created him or her to be, will be a delight to live with. And to be married to.

Isn't that what finding life in Christ did for us? In him, we experienced a new level of love, acceptance, and hope that pulled us toward a new life. Blessed. Joyful. Confident in God who takes notice of us and sees us as valuable—worth the price of his Son.

We are called as believers to build one another up, to encourage, and to *acknowledge* the lives of those around us. God formed us while we were yet in our mothers' wombs; God doesn't make junk. Our identity should never be built on what we've done, but on what he's done *in us*. That's a healthy sense of our worth. It doesn't mean we don't celebrate accomplishment. It means we are thankful to God who helped us achieve.

From that day on the tennis courts, Ron knew I acknowledged him and saw the great value God placed in him. When he discovered someone who was aware of his worth, it changed how he saw *himself*. Possibilities he never considered were now open to him. Small steps at first, but eventually long, confident strides toward the man God was calling him to be.

He was then, and is today, one of the greatest men I've ever known. He was a boy when I met him, and I have been present for the transformation. Watching God work has been amazing.

Why should we care about the self-worth of others, in this case, our spouses? It may help them walk as sons and daughters of the Most High God, so they can "run with endurance the race that is set before them" (Hebrews 12:1, paraphrased). One who is acknowledged, able to walk in the fullness of who God created him or her to be, will be a delight to live with. *And to be married to*.

Begin today to acknowledge the life of your loved one as God does. Build up; don't tear down. Speak highly of your spouse to others, and do it when he or she is present to hear. Be curious.

Discover the thoughts, ideas, and hopes that live in the head on that pillow next to yours. They might just surprise you.

> *Conventional wisdom: "Appreciation can make a day, even change a life. Your willingness to put it into words is all that is necessary."*
> —MARGARET COUSINS

Chapter 22 Choice Questions:
I Choose to Acknowledge You

1. Describe your spouse's level of self-worth. What is your loved one's view of his/her value?
2. What influences your spouse's self-view? Is it a healthy view? What experiences have shaped how your spouse sees himself/herself?
3. How can you strengthen your spouse's identity in Christ? What can you say or do?

Use the prayer below to declare your choice—or create one of your own.

Prayer: Father, please give me eyes to see my husband/wife as you do. Help me see the value you have placed on his/her life, so that I may walk with a recognition of that worth and reinforce it in what I say and do. I commit to building up, not tearing down, fully recognizing that my spouse is your child. I will help him/her overcome experiences that suggest worthlessness by reminding him/her of the truth in your Word. Thank you for your guidance as I choose today to acknowledge the one I am married to.

CHAPTER 23

I CHOOSE TO BELIEVE
IN YOU

*I'm sure about this: the one who started a good work in you
will stay with you to complete the job by the day of Christ Jesus.*
—PHILIPPIANS 1:6

How did this happen, Trent? You were doing so well; I just
don't get it." Tracy was in tears.

Trent's gaze was fixed on the carpet. He spoke without looking up. "I'm sorry, Trace. I never meant for this to happen."

"But it did happen! You've been clean for almost seven
months. You wouldn't even take the meds the doctor gave you
when you were so sick with the flu last summer. What led you
down that path again?"

"My back, Trace. You know how bad it's been since the accident. I could take it in the warm weather, but working outside
in the cold . . . I couldn't get through the day anymore." Trent
looked across the room at his wife. "Then you got laid off and
I couldn't afford to lose this job or miss any hours. Our heating

bill is through the roof, the fuel pump in the truck had to be replaced—and it's all on me. We could lose the house."

Tracy's face softened a bit. "I'm sorry it's put so much pressure on you, but Trent, we almost lost *us* when you were hooked on painkillers. Oxy nearly cost us our family—our life together."

"It's why I'm not hiding it anymore. I went to my boss today and told him I was going to need a couple weeks off." Trent could see the alarm on Tracy's face. "It's okay, babe. I prayed about it, and I knew it was the right thing to do. When Bert asked me why, I told him the truth. I thought he might fire me on the spot, but he was really cool about it. Turns out, he struggled with something similar after spinal surgery a couple of years ago."

Tracy relaxed a bit. "Well that's good. I'm proud of you for being upfront with him. But, what are we going to do? We can't afford rehab again."

Trent managed a hopeful smile. "Bert reminded me that our company has something called an employee assistance program that will cover rehab. I'll miss two weeks of pay, but he promised my job would be waiting when I come back. Even said he'd look into a new position that would put me inside in the cold weather. Tracy, I think this is God's way of helping me get clean for good."

"What do you mean?"

"Getting back into a small group at church was an important part of this. I wasn't just keeping it from you, but from our friends too. I'm so sorry I wasn't honest with you. Hiding it was killing me. Then last Sunday, Pastor Tom asked me to help with the teen ministry. I was excited but knew I had to say no. That was the final straw. God would not leave me alone about it. In fact, I stopped at the church and spoke to Pastor on my way home this afternoon. Told him what was going on and asked him to pray with me, to prepare me for this conversation. And Tracy, he agreed to be my accountability partner."

Tracy began to cry. "Trent, really? That's amazing."

"I guess that's why this feels like such a blow. God's been lighting a fire in my heart; I thought I was in such a good place." Trent looked down at his feet.

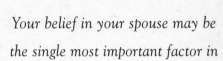

Your belief in your spouse may be the single most important factor in them believing in themselves.

"You *are* in a good place, babe—or at least in a better place than you've been before. You slipped, but you're back up and ready to fight this." Tracy moved to sit next to him on the couch. "You made some bad choices, but facing this head-on was the best choice you could have made."

Trent's accident and back injury created a challenge they never saw coming. A long, slow recovery led them on a journey that drained their bank account and left Trent with chronic pain, addicted to painkillers.

Tracy's been here before, disappointed and discouraged. It's easy to believe the race will be won when you've watched your spouse put discipline and determination into practice. But if you've seen him or her fall again and again, it's tough to have confidence that this time will be different. Is it even fair to expect it?

Probably not. But *fair* is not the point. The Bible instructs us to encourage, exhort, and love one another. "Most important of all, continue to show deep love for each other, for love covers a multitude of sins" (1 Peter 4:8 NLT). Becoming Christlike is a tall order.

I'm not suggesting it's okay for a husband or wife to live beyond the borders of reasonable behavior and demand love and acceptance. It's about the condition of the heart. Man looks at the outward appearance, but God looks at the heart.

Tracy's faith in God is strong. She can see the sorrow in Trent's eyes, knowing he let her down. She can also see a shift in his heart; there's a new spark of faith and determination. Her choice is clear.

"I'm not gonna lie—I'm disappointed, but I love you. You need to know I'm in your corner. We're going to fight this together—you, me, and the Lord." Tracy lifted his chin up toward her. "I forgive you, Trent James," she said softly. "And I believe you're going to beat this. *We're* going to beat this."

Trent pulled her close. "Father, help me to overcome this once and for all. I can do it only through your strength and her support. We believe you can move mountains if we will have even a tiny bit of faith. Thank you, Lord, for a wife who has faith in you and is willing to believe in me."

Tracy smiled as she looked into her husband's eyes. "Amen!"

> *Conventional wisdom: "God puts people in our lives on purpose so we can help them succeed and help them become all he created them to be. Most people will not reach their full potential without somebody else believing in them."*
> —JOEL OSTEEN

Chapter 23 Choice Questions:
I Choose to Believe in You

1. What has your spouse attempted but failed to achieve? What would your spouse like to accomplish but hasn't even attempted? What's the impact on him/her? On you?

2. Do you believe in your spouse's ability to accomplish these things? Are you walking by faith or by sight? What can you do to express your belief in a meaningful way?

3. Commit to praying each day for your husband or. wife and yourself. Look up these scriptures; write them out in your journal or on sticky notes placed where you will be reminded of them. Include them in your prayers.

   - Hebrews 11:1
   - Romans 8:37
   - 2 Corinthians 5:7
   - Matthew 18:19

Use the prayer below to declare your choice—or create one of your own.

Prayer: Your Word declares that faith is the substance of things we hope for, the evidence of things we cannot see. I choose to stand on your Word and believe in my spouse. I will not allow the enemy to accuse him/her by reminding me of past failures or difficulties. I will choose to encourage my spouse when self-doubt creeps in for either of us, and I will pray daily *with* and *for* my loved one. When either of us is tempted to throw in the towel, I choose to continue by faith, believing that you, Lord, will move mountains.

CHAPTER 24

I CHOOSE TO HELP YOU ACHIEVE YOUR DREAMS AND GOALS

Hope deferred makes the heart sick, but a dream fulfilled is a tree of life.

—Proverbs 13:12 (NLT)

"You want to do *what?*" she asked.

He smiled and cleared his throat. "I want to start my own business."

"You want to quit your job, give up your benefits, surrender security for our family, and start a business of your own. Is that it?" she demanded.

It was something he'd never mentioned before. This discussion landed on her like a wolf at the door.

She was a stay-at-home mom five years now. They had three sons, a mortgage, and two car payments. Little boys needed soccer uniforms and the roof needed replacing. *Didn't he see how impossible this was?*

He broke through her thoughts. "I feel God's behind this desire. I do believe it's his idea," he continued. "But I'd never make this decision on my own. And I will not do it without your agreement," he reassured her.

The roaring in her ears began to quiet, and her heart ceased its pounding.

"Let me tell you about my ideas and what I want to do so we can discuss it and pray together, asking for God's direction."

He had done his research. His plans were well defined. His rationale was solid. The family was at the very heart of the concept: he desired to have more time to spend with them and the autonomy to set his own schedule so he could coach the boys' teams and go on school field trips. And he was in no hurry. But perhaps most important—he wanted to hear her thoughts and concerns.

Working together to remove obstacles and overcome the things that may stand in the way can make one person's dream an exciting joint venture.

She spoke with her friend, who reminded her of the many times her husband had supported her. "Isn't this the guy who made certain that you got to pursue just about everything you ever dreamed of?" the friend asked. *True*, she admitted to herself.

"Without your agreement, he is not willing to move forward. You owe him this opportunity," her friend continued. "You'll always wonder what God might have done."

So she made a list. He listened. He agreed that her concerns were valid and would have to be addressed. She immediately relaxed.

"Would you pray with me?" he asked. "Would you stand with me to ask God to reveal his will? And if this is what he wants for us, for our family, we will trust him to show us how and when to move forward. He can show us how to deal with the items on *our* list." He had accepted shared ownership; it was no longer *her* list.

They prayed and, over time, both were confident that God was moving them in this new and somewhat frightening direction. They sought counsel from God and from godly advisors to whom the Lord directed them. And *then* they created a plan. They set goals both of them could get behind, and they tackled them one at a time, pulling together to support what had been *his* dream, which had now become *their* dream.

One year later, every item on the list had been checked off. He had met her need for security by working his regular job while starting his business part-time at nights and on weekends—which allowed them to bank six months of expenses. Once accomplished, he quit his job and officially launched the highly successful business that would endure for fifteen years, until he entered the ministry.

It was only a few short years after he began his business that the Lord began to alter his plan for her career as well, and she set out to establish a company of her own. With her husband's full agreement and commitment to *her* goals and dreams.

But this time was easier. She was open and excited about what lay ahead. God had a good track record with these two, and their faith has grown as they've seen God fulfill his Word. Here they go again. In him, they can dare to dream.

> *Conventional wisdom: "It takes a lot of courage to show your dreams to someone else."*
> —ERMA BOMBECK

Chapter 24 Choice Questions:
I Choose to Help You Achieve Your Dreams
and Goals

1. What's the dream that your spouse desires to pursue? Career, hobby, special interest, education, ministry, financial?
2. Are the two of you in agreement in pursuit of the dream? Why or why not?
3. What's standing in the way? How can you help make it possible?
4. What can you choose to do today to support this dream? What steps can you agree to take together?

Use the prayer below to declare your choice—or create one of your own.

Prayer: Father, I choose to dream with my spouse and find a place of agreement to pursue as a goal together. We will not move forward without unity and will move only as you direct. Please help me voice my concerns and any reservations or fears I may have about this goal in a way that builds my spouse's understanding. Lord, help us remove obstacles and overcome the things that may stand in our way. I desire to hear your voice and will submit to your direction. I pray that you will make your will clear to both of us and help us to operate within your timing, knowing that it may require patience to do it your way.

I CHOOSE TO CELEBRATE
YOUR SUCCESS

Be happy with those who are happy, and cry with those who are crying.

—Romans 12:15

Oh, you must be Mr. Deb!" Alicia extended her hand to my husband. "We've all heard a lot about you. Your wife is the best boss we've ever had!"

Ron smiled. I tried, but struggled to maintain a pleasant expression. *I can't believe she called him Mr. Deb! But he's acting as though it was nothing out of the ordinary. Thank you, Lord, for a gracious man.* We chatted a while longer with Alicia and then moved on at my company's holiday party.

"I'm so sorry, babe," I said as we headed toward the food table. "I think she was just trying to be cute. She's so young, I'm sure she didn't realize how it might have landed. She's heard me talk about you a million times, and trust me, she *knows* your name."

"It's not a big deal, Deb. She was eager to tell me how much she enjoys working for you and about the great changes you've made. It made me so proud to hear that you are really making a difference for her and the others on your team. She said you were a real inspiration." He snickered a little, but I could see he was enjoying himself. "At least all the long hours you've put in are paying off." He squeezed my hand. *He really is happy for me.*

I shot him one of those silent *thank-you* messages as I saw my boss approaching. I tightened my grip on his hand. "Oh, Deb! This must be your hubby! I'm so glad to meet you," Dan said as he pumped Ron's hand. "Your wife's been a great addition to our team. We all feel mighty lucky to have her…"

God has blessed my life in so many ways. My career is one of the areas God has shown himself to be faithful. Although I never finished college, I was promoted quickly and often into jobs that usually required a degree. I worked very hard, but I have no illusions that I built the success alone. I knew God's favor was on me, even as it was happening.

I also knew my husband was my biggest cheerleader. Always supportive. Always helping me pray through some issue or problem at work. And when I felt God tugging on me to start my own business, Ron was the first to jump on that bandwagon. In fact, he drove it—he was the one to suggest it to me. And he was always ready to assist in any way I needed. "Someday I'll have a job I can do all by myself," I laughingly said after he helped me pull off yet another tough assignment. "I wouldn't count on it," he said. But he laughed along with me.

And then two years ago, God added ministry to my plate. The call to write and speak on the Lord's behalf was something I had not foreseen in my life. I didn't choose it; God chose it for me. It meant some changes in our routine, since I was still running my business full-time. More nights and weekends at the computer for me. More meals and laundry on Ron's list. But each little encouragement—an article printed, a request for a book proposal—was a joint celebration.

When I landed my first book contract, Ron danced me through the hallway of our home. And he sat with a big grin on his face, smiling proudly, when the applause was for me during the launch party for that book. He's driven me hundreds of miles to media interviews and brainstormed material when I've had momentary writer's block.

Success is so much sweeter when it's shared. And when it's shared with the one with whom you are one, the celebration is rich indeed.

He's held down the fort when I was away at conferences and trotted to the post office, the office supply, and the printer on short notice.

He's absolutely right. I can't do the job without him. And I don't plan to try.

Ron's never lived a moment in my shadow, nor I in his. I've applauded and celebrated his achievements, as he has mine. We've each had our time at center stage, but we always shared the spotlight. Those who have seen me post a win know I credit Ron for the key role he plays. It's been a partnership. God. Ron. And me. The Word reminds us that a three-stranded cord is not easily broken (Ecclesiastes 4:12). For us, it's been the key. Anything we may accomplish is only because of God's goodness, and any praise it receives belongs to the Lord.

I do appreciate the help—all the practical and emotional support Ron's provided. But even more important to me is that he's genuinely happy about my success. There's never been a hint of "Oh, what's the big deal?" He's celebrated every triumph with genuine enthusiasm, and his friends tell me he brags on me shamelessly.

Success is so much sweeter when it's shared. And when it's shared with the one with whom *you* are one, the celebration is rich indeed.

Will you support the success of your spouse? Will you set aside the frustration of your own thwarted goals to applaud your spouse's achievements? What will you choose today?

> *Conventional wisdom: "One of the sanest, surest, and most generous joys of life comes from being happy over the good fortune of others."*
> —Robert A. Heinlein

Chapter 25 Choice Questions:
I Choose to Celebrate Your Success

1. How do you feel when your spouse is successful? What's the impact on you?
2. Do you ever feel a twinge of envy or sadness for your own stalled accomplishment? If so, how can you move past your frustration to join in the celebration?
3. Success often starts with very small wins. How can you encourage your spouse to continue toward the goal? What roadblocks can you help him/her overcome?
4. How can you celebrate your spouse's success in a manner that is meaningful to him/her?

Use the prayer below to declare your choice—or create one of your own.

Prayer: Today I pray for the ability to rejoice with my spouse when he/she is successful. I ask your Spirit to help me leave personal envy and jealousy behind, so I will not covet the acknowledgment that comes with my mate's success. I commit to rejoice with my beloved and not compete for the attention offered in honor of the accomplishment. I commit to a full heart of celebration when my spouse succeeds. I choose to celebrate!

CHAPTER 26

I CHOOSE TO INVEST IN YOU

Instead of each person watching out for their own good,
watch out for what is better for others.
—Philippians 2:4

The conference brochures were lying on the table when he came home. He was not particularly surprised to see them.

She didn't waste any time, Ron thought to himself. *When she gets an idea and a green light from God, she punches the gas pedal.* It made him smile; how well he understood the way I'm wired. He's spent a lifetime of learning me.

We had been high school sweethearts, neither of us finishing college before the wedding bells rang. We never regretted it, but there *had* been missed opportunities here and there as a result. We each became successful in our careers—the combination of God's favor and our hard work seemed to smooth over the lack of degrees. We each owned a successful business.

I am an avid learner, will always be a lifelong student. I value conferences and classes—I am interested in anything that might help me build my knowledge or career. Ron had always been onboard, gladly accepting the responsibility of a week alone with the kids and the additional expense. No problem.

But this time was different.

Over the years I had often been asked the same question, "When are you going to write your book?" Ron, in fact, was the first to recognize the gift, and as a result, asked me about it often. My brother, a journalist, saw it too and suggested I take a crack at it. A longtime friend told me the same thing. But I had dismissed it. "It's not what I do," I had responded impatiently to her after yet another inquiry.

"It's not what you do? Or it's not what you've done?" she asked. "They're not the same, you know. God gave you a gift for a purpose. You've used it effectively in your business for years, but someday he's going to call that in for the kingdom's benefit."

Investing spiritually, emotionally, and financially in your spouse's gifts and calling will offer a greater return than you ever imagined.

That statement stopped me in my tracks. I had never considered God might have given me the ability to write for anything *other* than business. Was the gift given to fulfill God's calling in my life to expand his kingdom? That had never occurred to me. I prayed. God said yes.

I talked about it with Ron (who said, "Finally!"). Both of us were excited to see a new chapter unfold in my life. There was much to learn, and I discovered it was not as easy as sitting down at the keyboard, tapping away. Hence, the conference brochures on the table.

"When are you leaving?" Ron asked.

"Where am I going?"

"The writer's conference in San Antonio. When are you leaving?" He smiled at me indulgently. I love that smile.

Immediately the details, the excitement, and the chatter began. *Familiar to him, all familiar.*

There was travel and conference fees and rental car expense. "Go," he said. I was beyond grateful and promised to work very hard, which he knew would be the case. His support as I began this new adventure created confidence. I treasured knowing he prayed for me. It was one more way in which he helped me develop the talent and gift God placed in me.

In fact, there are three areas in which Ron invested in me as I answered God's call.

1. *He invested in me spiritually.* He believed God would use me. Ron had seen the gift, long before I did. It was evident to him and God confirmed it. Why was he able to spot it? Because he regarded me not only as his wife but also as a spiritual being with a unique calling. We often prayed together that God would use us for his purposes. Once that purpose was confirmed for me, Ron called it out by mentioning it frequently, planting the seed in my heart. He was confident God desired that seed to grow.

2. *He invested in me emotionally.* Ron listened (endlessly) to me read one revision after another as I worked my way through an article or chapter. He provided feedback, even

if I wasn't always gracious about his perspective. He brainstormed with me, and on more than one occasion, his biblical knowledge provided a critical component I needed. Ron encouraged me when publishers said, "No thanks," and he rejoiced when a magazine article was accepted for publication. He bragged about my writing to others, which always got back to me through friends. Ron was in my corner, and I knew it. I felt it.

3. *He invested in me financially.* Conferences, software, and a coach were just a few of the investments required to develop my writing. It meant eating out would be more of a treat and vacations less lavish. It cost us something to follow God, but we had long lived with the belief that investment leads to increase. This was no exception.

The increase did come. Within a year of answering the call, I sold my first book to a Christian publishing house. By the end of the second year, book one was published with two more under contract. I have been published several times by an international Christian women's magazine, and I am a monthly columnist for one of the largest Christian periodical publishers in the world. God is so good.

How important was Ron in the process? More important than he may ever know. He could have squelched it, simply by withholding his investment of time, talent, and treasure.

Today I am walking in the call God envisioned for my life when he formed me in my mother's womb. It's a level of fulfillment I never anticipated and, until now, never experienced in my work. And to think I almost missed it because it wasn't what I'd ever done before.

Conventional wisdom: "Transformation in the world happens when people are healed and start investing in other people."

—Michael W. Smith

Chapter 26 Choice Questions:
I Choose to Invest in You

1. What is your spouse called to do? What are the goals and dreams that need your support? Have you invested in them? Why or why not?

2. What investments are you currently making to bring those pursuits to reality?

3. How can you invest spiritually, emotionally, and financially? List the specific things you can do, beginning today.

Use the prayer below to declare your choice—or create one of your own.

Prayer: Father, thank you for investing in my life by sending your Son, Jesus—the most priceless sacrifice of all. You are generous with your children, and you have demonstrated that principle again and again in my life. I desire to invest in those things that are important to my spouse, whether they are of a business nature, a personal goal, or to fulfill a spiritual call or desire. I ask your Spirit to lead me to a clear understanding of what I can and should invest emotionally, spiritually, and financially to help those dreams become a reality. Guide me to be a good steward with my investment and help me to be patient in the process without demanding a return on my timeline. I will trust you for the increase.

I CHOOSE TO COMFORT YOU

Therefore comfort each other and edify one another, just as you also are doing.

—1 Thessalonians 5:11 NKJV

Bonnie woke at 4:00 a.m. with what her doctor calls "breakthrough anxiety." She told her friends it is in the wee hours, when her defenses are down, that her heart breaks with the continued absence of her grandson, Charlie, from her and her husband's lives. "Christmas without him is tough, to say the least," she admits.

"Last night when I woke up, I made no noise; my eyes were closed in the darkness when I heard Mark ask, 'Are you okay? Do you need me to hold you?'"

"How did you know I wasn't okay?" Bonnie asked, finally letting weeks of pent-up tears fall.

"Husbands know these things," he told her.

Awake now, Mark went downstairs and returned with two steaming mugs in hand. "I made you a cup of coffee, and in case it's too strong, I also brought some hot water to dilute it with," he said as he sat down beside her.

Bonnie says, "I will never get over being treated so tenderly by a loving man...it still slays and surprises me, even after a decade of a delightful marriage."

When we hurt, we need comfort.

Hurt comes from a variety of places. Family issues, like the one Bonnie and Mark are experiencing, are often at the top of the parental list of pain. Worry over financial concerns, health issues, and dealing with aging parents are a just a few additional ways we become wounded or fearful. It's a long list of possibilities.

It's okay to need someone to lean on or cry with, someone to pray for you when you are weak. Comfort covers us like an old quilt. It gathers us up and tucks us in.

God is always our first line of defense in dealing with our hurts. He is, after all, the Comforter. His Word reminds us in 2 Corinthians 1:3 "Blessed *be* the God and Father of our Lord Jesus Christ, the Father of mercies and God of *all comfort*" (NKJV, emphasis mine).

The Word of the Lord is able to calm our concern and quiet our anxiety. We know he is there, and he never leaves us or turns us over to the wave that threatens to swallow us in sorrow. *But there are moments* when we need a physical touch, arms to encircle us, someone's presence to soothe us. Someone to bring us coffee in the middle of the night.

What is comfort? How do you provide it? It might be as simple as someone praying over us or with us. Perhaps a listener, intent on understanding how we feel in a difficult time without the need to give advice or solve our problem. And the simple, quiet presence of another during times of hurt can be the most soothing of all; the knowledge that another cares enough to be silently near, at the ready, on standby should we cry out in distress or call for help.

How do you know when to act and what to do? Pray. God's Spirit is ever-present in each situation. The Lord knows our very thoughts and will show us how and when to comfort others. Knowing your spouse's moods and patterns will provide you clues as well. Quieter than usual? Angry over what seems trivial? Check in. There may be a need you can address.

One of the mistakes we often make when we support loved ones in need of comfort is to take the actions that we ourselves would find comforting. For example, if I prefer to draw away from others to sort out my emotions, my preference is to have someone nearby but not offering advice or asking me questions about what's wrong. That works for me; it may not be the painkiller for my spouse. What to do? Here are a few things to keep in mind:

- Be an encourager. Sometimes it's easier to communicate your comfort to your spouse through a quick, handwritten note or card to let them know you are supporting them in their struggle. Slip it under her pillow or into his lunchbox. Even a text during the day that says, "I'm praying for you," can be an encouragement.

- Be patient. Helping folks work through their pain cannot be rushed. Your need for them to find their way to the

other side comes across as you push the pace of their process. We get there when we get there.

• Be willing to let them direct the traffic. If you are unsure
which path to take, simply ask, "How can I help you?"

We may be embarrassed to reach out when we are in pain.
It's okay to need someone to lean on or cry with, someone to
pray for you when you are weak. Comfort covers us like an old
quilt. It gathers us up and tucks us in. It relieves our aching and
soothes the pain. It warms us and restores hope.

Remember that two is better than one, for if one falls down,
he has the other to help him up. Or to bring him coffee in the
middle of the night.

*Conventional wisdom: "Remember, we all stumble, every
one of us. That's why it's a comfort to go hand-in-hand."*
—EMILY KIMBROUGH

Chapter 27 Choice Questions:
I Choose to Comfort You

1. What comforts you? What can others do to make you feel cared for during difficult times?
2. What comforts your spouse? It's dangerous to assume that the same actions you find comforting will soothe your spouse in the same way. If you are unsure, ask!
3. How do you know when your spouse is in need of comfort? What are the signs and symptoms he/she is hurting?
4. What brings your spouse to the breaking point? What hurts or concerns create anxiety or pain? What opportunities do you have to offer comfort? How will you do that—starting today?

Use the prayer below to declare your choice—or create one of your own.

Prayer: Father, you are the Comforter, and you live in me. I desire to bring hope to the one I love when hopelessness invades. I want to provide assurance when there is anxiousness, and peace when panic threatens to overwhelm my spouse's soul. Help me to be sensitive to the signs that hurt or pain is present, and show me the best way to be a comforting presence. I will not wait until my spouse sounds the alarm or until things spiral. I need not have advice or understanding, but I choose to be present and follow as your Spirit leads, offering silence or encouragement—available but not hovering—and prayer that soothes the broken heart.

CHAPTER 28

I CHOOSE TO LIVE
IN PEACE WITH YOU

*If possible, to the best of your ability, live at peace with all
people.*

—Romans 12:18

"So, am I off the hook yet, or am I still on your bad list?" Annie
asked Paul. He didn't look up.

No response.

"How much longer can you walk around the house pretend-
ing I'm not here? It's been nearly two days, Paul. Haven't I been
punished long enough?" Annie could feel her anger boiling all
over again. "I've said I'm sorry. I know I was wrong. You win!
You've made your point."

Paul looked up from his book. "It's not about winning. And
I heard you, this time and the four or five other times you apol-
ogized, Annie. What you did hurt me. It caught me off-guard,"
Paul replied. "I'm not sure how long it's going to take to let it go.
Until then, it's better to limit our conversation so it doesn't all

spiral out of control again." With that, Paul put down his book and headed for the garage.

Someone eavesdropping might assume Paul and Annie are having a fight. They'd be wrong. Annie accepted responsibility for her actions and apologized for the hurt she caused. Paul *said* he'd forgiven her when she asked him to do so. The fight is over. It's been over for forty-eight hours. This is the *aftermath* of the fight.

The offender is contrite, but apparently the sentence is not yet up.

When we marry, we become one. That's God's plan. It's not an easy plan to live twenty-four hours a day, 365 days a year. A marriage is between two people with two experiences and two perspectives, working to fashion one heart and a life together that pleases God. Sometimes marriage is loud and there's bumping into one another in the process. But it can be a very healthy part of our life together.

Relationships can be fragile things. They are easily damaged and sometimes broken for a number of reasons:

- We insist on our own way.
- We say hurtful things in the heat of the moment.
- We are critical, cranky, and crabby—and we take it out on others.
- We keep score, rehash old arguments, hold grudges, and nurse wounds.

And that's a partial list. Any of it sound familiar? We are human, and this is humanity at its worst. Not attractive, is it?

Conflict in marriage is inevitable. Fighting fair is not. It takes intentional strategy to fight fair.

Rules for fighting? You'd better have rules! One of the most important guidelines is that when it's over—it's over. It's the missing piece for Paul and Annie. Amends have been made, apologies offered, and forgiveness requested and granted. Paul has genuinely released the offense in his head. But his heart has not quite caught up. Forgiveness that comes with the silent treatment *because I'm not quite ready to let you forget about what you did to me* is allowing your feelings to guide your course of action. That's troubled turf.

Aren't you glad it's not the example Jesus set?

Face it, we aren't quite at his level yet. *Forgive and forget* is easier to say than to do, yet that's not what God requires. We must be willing to let unity be restored. By holding your spouse at arm's length, swathed in silence, you've blocked the path to peace.

Conflict in marriage is inevitable. Fighting fair is not. It takes intentional strategy to fight fair.

Annie has catapulted through a carnival of emotions since the original argument. The silent treatment has taken her from remorseful to resentful. She's now feeling angry over Paul's management of his feelings and is unclear about what more she can do but to wait it out. She wants it to be over.

And God's Word agrees. "Do not let the sun go down on your wrath" (Ephesians 4:26 NKJV).

God instructs us to deal with our upset *without delay*. At least not beyond the end of the day. He wants resolution and restoration for us, but it doesn't happen unless we can summon the courage to *let it go* once it's over. We must *choose* to live in peace with one another. And if that peace is difficult to find, ask the Lord to give you some of his. It's the peace that passes all human understanding.

God is the master of creating peace in relationships. His direction to deal with hurt, conflict, and anger before the end of the day is designed to protect us. Will the negative feelings vanish immediately? Probably not, but entertaining them and allowing them to define our actions is dangerous. The feelings will fester and infect the heart and the mind.

When we withdraw, refusing to allow healing to take place, peace is nowhere to be found. But it is in the silence that the enemy's whispers find our listening ear. He accuses others and bolsters our indignation. It does not take long for the chasm to widen and the hurt to be reignited.

Refuse to be a partner with the father of lies by finding the strength in the Spirit of the Lord to let it go.

Release the hostage; choose peace. Here are a few tips to make that possible:

- *Create closure*. Apologize for your role in the conflict and any hurt you may have caused. Ask for forgiveness—from your spouse and from God.
- *Pray*. Together if your spouse is willing; alone if he or she is not. Make a declaration to move forward and let it go.
- *Actively re-engage*. Do something together to help your love override the feelings that prompt punishment instead of peace. A walk, an evening out—any activity that helps rekindle the connection.

I challenge you to delay no longer. Today, make a choice for peace.

Conventional Wisdom: *"Peace is not something you wish for; it's something you make, something you do, something you are, and something you give away."*
—ROBERT FULGHUM

Chapter 28 Questions:
I Choose to Live in Peace with You

1. How well do you handle the aftermath of an argument with your spouse? Are you a peacemaker or a punisher? What about your spouse? What's the impact of your approach on your relationship?
2. What steps do you and your spouse take to create closure and move on? What steps are you willing to take?

Use the prayer below to declare your choice—or create one of your own.

Prayer: Lord, I desire to honor your Word and to live at peace with everyone, including my husband/wife. I accept your instruction to deal with hurt, anger, and conflict swiftly, and I believe it is designed to protect me personally, in addition to our relationship as husband and wife. I refuse to partner with Satan and will not entertain accusations against my spouse, or permit the enemy to question the stability of our marriage with his lies. I choose to let go of the hurt or anger that conflict has created and will not punish or penalize my mate through silence or withdrawal. Holy Spirit, I ask that you help me by reminding me to choose peace.

CHAPTER 29

I CHOOSE TO SUPPORT YOU

Two people are better off than one, for they can help each other succeed.

—Ecclesiastes 4:9 (NLT)

There's a message from your mom on the answering machine," Kaley said to Tim as he looked through the stack of mail on the counter. "She'd like you to come for dinner after church on Sunday."

Tim looked up. "Tomorrow? Are we busy?"

"I said she'd like *you* to come to dinner. I wasn't included in the invitation," Kaley responded softly. "I just don't understand why she doesn't like me. Will she ever accept me as your wife? We've been married nearly a year and she's been pretty clear about how she feels."

Tim dropped the mail on the coffee table and crossed the room to put his arm around Kaley. "I'm so sorry, babe. I've been clear too. If you're not invited, I'm not going. I told her the last time this happened that it's *both* of us—or *neither* of us."

"Listen to the message. It's her birthday on Tuesday. All she wants for her birthday is a chance to have dinner with her only son. Can you really say no, given the situation?" Kaley looked up at Tim. He nodded reassuringly.

"I can, and I will. I don't need to listen to the message. This time it's *her* birthday, then it will be *my* birthday...there will always be a good reason in her mind for it to be just the two of us. She knows where I stand on this. If you're not welcome, neither am I."

Tim's mom is a single parent who raised Tim alone. His dad was out of the picture from the time he was a toddler. As a result, he and his mom have always been very close. Tim loves his mom and knows she is lonely. He would be glad to visit her. But the woman is open about her feelings for Kaley: *You are not my daughter, and I am not interested in a relationship with you.* For Tim, that's a deal breaker.

Kaley is grateful for Tim's support, but there's no feeling of victory here. "I hope someday we can all sit down together as a family. Birthdays, holidays, regular days. Do you think that will ever happen?"

Tim shrugged. "I don't know, Kaley, but here's what I do know: I won't let her manipulate the situation to exclude you. Not this time, not ever. We're a package deal."

Family relationships can be tricky. Kaley is fortunate her husband is clear about the biblical principles for marriage. "This explains why a man leaves his father and mother and is joined to his wife, and the two are united into one" (Genesis 2:24 NLT). Tim's position not only supports his wife, it honors God as well. It's a difficult thing to do, but he is willing to take a stand.

Support can come in many ways. When I was desperate to leave a job that had become a nightmare, Ron was in it with me; first, by talking it over, then by praying with me to seek God's direction. And when it was clearly time to resign, he encouraged me to do it without delay, even though it would create some financial challenges for a while. I backed him when he started his business, and he encourages me in my writing activities.

Support your spouse wherever and whenever it's needed. Success is always more easily achieved when you stand together.

Support does not always have to be a grand gesture or a big deal. Simply taking interest in the things your spouse enjoys or is involved in is a great way to show it. I remember one time Ron walked the sales floor with me at a big show for knitters. He was one of only a few guys present, each giving one another sympathetic looks as they passed.

For parenting couples, kids need and deserve consistent guidelines, rules, and methods of discipline. Once parents decide on a course of action on an issue, problem, or privilege, they both must uphold that decision, stand behind it and each other. When Mom overrules Dad and lets a child off the hook, she is failing to support her husband. Children will learn to use this inconsistency to their advantage, and in so doing, upset the balance of a parent-led home.

The dictionary reminds us that the word *support* is a verb—it requires action. The dictionary details a set of actions when defining the word: advocate, assist, bear, comfort, corroborate, encourage, exhort, help, and reinforce. That's a long list of steps, and they all go beyond simply sympathizing or thinking favorably when someone is in need.

You can support your spouse in many ways. A few examples:

- Help him or her deal with criticism that's been hurtful. Talk it over and sort through whether it's baseless or valid. If it's valid, speak the truth in love. Your spouse may be more open to hearing it from you than someone else.
- Encourage your spouse to pursue an interest, job opportunity, or new venture.
- Attend a sports event for his favorite team or a charity fashion show she's helped put together, even though you'd rather be doing something else.
- Be present when your spouse loses a friend or loved one. There are benefits to having your husband or wife near, willing to listen to the stories, the tears, or the anger at losing someone close.

As Kaley and Tim experienced, support may come in the form of standing up for your spouse. Action is required when he or she is excluded, attacked, or inappropriately treated by another person—family member or otherwise. You are on sure footing when you allow the Bible to define your actions, behaviors, and decisions. Tim has been firm but loving with his mom.

The support Tim provides Kaley helps them stay strong and united as a couple, and Kaley is confident of her husband's commitment.

The good news is that Tim's persistence in resisting attempts to exclude his wife is beginning to pay off. His mom recently asked the couple to join her at a concert. They accepted the invitation quickly and were surprised at what a great time they all had together. Progress!

Conventional Wisdom: *"Support the people you love and be there for them. Flaws and all."*
—UNKNOWN

Chapter 29 Choice Questions:
I Choose to Support You

1. What issues is your spouse struggling with where support would be helpful? What activities or hobbies could you support with your presence, encouragement, or interest?
2. What kind of support would be most helpful? If you are uncertain, ask!
3. What will you do to stand with your husband or wife?

Use the prayer below to declare your choice—or create one of your own.

Prayer: Ecclesiastes 4:12 says: "A person standing alone can be attacked and defeated, but two can stand back-to-back and conquer. Three are even better, for a triple-braided cord is not easily broken" (NLT). Father, my goal is to support my spouse wherever and whenever it's needed. Success is always more easily achieved when we stand together; and only when we stand, hidden in you, can we be certain that we are in your will. I ask your Spirit to show me how to best support my loved one and reveal the steps I should take. Today I choose to walk in your steps.

CHAPTER 30

I CHOOSE TO PRAY FOR YOU

The prayer of the righteous person is powerful in what it can achieve.

—JAMES 5:16

Alison walked out of the room without looking at Phil's new leather jacket. She was really upset. *Are you kidding me? A leather jacket! There's $250 we didn't have to spend. I don't get it. How can he be so clueless?*

Phil stood with the bag still in his hand and watched Alison head down the hall. No angry words. No "you'll just have to return it." She retreated quietly to the bedroom and closed the door, looking as if she might cry. *That's new*, he thought. He was prepared with his argument—how it had been on clearance, a really great savings over the original price. But he never had the chance.

Alison believes Phil has turned a deaf ear to her when it comes to their finances. She put a lot of effort into creating budget spreadsheets for each month and felt better with the numbers predetermined in the payment categories, but Phil barely looked at them. He pretended to listen, but nothing changed. She had tried, unsuccessfully, to shame him into attending the financial stewardship class at church with her, reminding him of the pile of past-due bills. He humored her by agreeing to read the book she received at the class. *I think he leafed through the pages without really reading any of it at all*, she thought. *I have to find a way to make him see this.*

Making people see things your way or do something they don't want to do—especially your husband or wife—is nearly impossible. It doesn't keep us from trying, though. You'd think we'd learn it's a losing proposition.

The stress and strain on a marriage is overwhelming when couples fail to share values, goals, or priorities. He wants to spend; she wants to save. She wants to go on vacation; he wants to use the money for home repairs. We can expend enormous energy working to convince, persuade, or cajole our mate into seeing things our way, and the outcome is often frustration, anger, and a divided home.

Why is prayer often the last resort—as the only thing left after we've tried everything else? God can accomplish what we cannot.

While Alison and Phil don't need to agree on every detail, unity in their situation is important. And Alison is running out of ideas to convince Phil of the need to make some changes. *I guess the only thing left to do is pray*, she thought as she picked at the stray threads of the worn comforter.

Why is prayer often considered a last resort? As the only thing left after we've tried everything else? Is it possible that God can accomplish what we cannot?

Debate, nagging, complaining, threatening, or begging will never come close to the power of prayer. Jesus promised, "Whatever you ask in my name, this I will do, that the Father may be glorified in the Son" (John 14:13 ESV).

I watched my mother-in-law pray faithfully for nearly thirty years for her husband, Mel, to come to the Lord. She lived her life fully devoted to God, and it broke her heart that Mel was not open to discuss his salvation with her. He gave her very little encouragement in this, and to most of us, it seemed a lost cause. She never gave up believing, though, and she never stopped praying. She was confident God would answer her prayer and never seemed frustrated or impatient with Mel or with God. She modeled Philippians 4:6-7: "Don't worry about anything; instead, pray about everything. Tell God what you need, and thank him for all he has done. Then you will experience God's peace, which exceeds anything we can understand. His peace will guard your hearts and minds as you live in Christ Jesus" (NLT). Ultimately God rewarded the time she spent on her knees, and the last few years of their lives together brought unparalleled joy.

Alison longed for a similar unity in her marriage. Her heart and mind craved for peace over their finances. Worry robbed her of joy and added to the anxiety she experienced. Finally she hit the wall. Nothing left to do but pray.

God, I give it all to you. You know our situation. I can no longer try to be Phil's Holy Spirit. He needs to hear from you, and so do I . . .

The door opened slowly. Phil was surprised to see her kneeling at the side of the bed. Alison looked up and caught Phil's expression; he looked concerned. She smiled and took a deep breath. *Okay, God. It's in your hands.*

> *Conventional wisdom: "The battle for our lives, and the lives and souls of our children, our husbands, our friends, our families, our neighbors, and our nation is waged on our knees."*
> —STORMIE OMARTIAN

Chapter 30 Choice Questions:
I Choose to Pray for You

1. In what areas are you and your spouse lacking agreement? What divisions create concern, tension, or anger between you?

2. How often do you pray for your mate? What can you do to make it a regular practice?

3. Set a time to pray daily for your husband or wife. Consider the following areas: physical needs, emotional needs, and spiritual needs.

   • What goals does your spouse have that you can support in prayer?

   • What needs do you have as a couple that concern you, your spouse, or both of you?

   • What areas would you like to see your husband/wife develop in that may be accomplished, not by your coaching, but by prayer?

Use the prayer below to declare your choice—or create one of your own.

Prayer: Father, I choose to stand on the power of prayer and the truth of your Word by praying for my mate according to Philippians 4:6-7. I will not worry about anything; instead, I choose to pray about everything. Lord, I bring you my needs, and I thank you for all you have done. Only then will I experience your peace, which exceeds anything I can understand. Your peace will guard my heart and mind as I live in Christ Jesus. Open our listening ears to hear the voice of your Spirit. I know you will bring us an answer, and I trust that we will hear a unified response, whether for healing, forgiveness, salvation, direction, or unity. I trust wholly in you.

CHAPTER 31

I CHOOSE TO PREFER YOU

Submit to each other out of respect for Christ.
—Ephesians 5:21

What a long couple of days! Driving 350 miles in twenty-four hours will wear you out.

When we finally arrived home, I remembered there were e-mails awaiting responses and a proposal I promised to write for a client. Finding focus sufficient to complete the tasks required coffee. And chocolate.

My husband worked a bit on his laptop in the den adjacent to my office. About ten o'clock he announced he was beat—and heading to bed. "Are you coming?" Ron asked.

"I'll be along soon," I said. "Shouldn't be too long." I almost believed it myself. I could hear the sleepy rhythm of his breathing within a few minutes. *Must be nice.*

Three and a half hours later, eyes heavy-lidded, I turned off the light. It was past 1:00 A.M. *Crazy,* I thought. Then I remembered the suitcase, with the things I needed before I went to bed. I wasn't even certain we'd dragged the doggone bag in from the car. And I wasn't interested in heading out into the cold dark night to retrieve it. *Guess I'm sleeping in a t-shirt.* Then I remembered the nighttime medication safely tucked into the side pocket of my travel case. *Ugh. No choice. I have to have it.*

I followed the sound of soft snoring down the hallway and padded quietly into our bedroom, trying not to waken Ron. He had left the small lamp lit at my side of the bed. There was the suitcase, sitting on our little luggage stand. It was open, and I could see that he had moved some things around. I then spotted my pajamas on the foot of the bed, where he had also spread my favorite quilt. A fresh bottle of water had been placed next to my medication on my nightstand. *That's my man.*

It might seem like a very small, almost insignificant gesture, but it's not. Ron knows my writing pattern—when I get started, it can pull me in and hold me captive for hours. He knew how tired I'd be when I finally surfaced, and even though he was also exhausted, he took the extra time to make my bedtime routine as quick and simple for me as possible. It's one of the things I love about him. It's one of the things that *made* me fall in love with him thirty-eight years ago.

> *Christ's example of sacrificial living serves as our pattern. Living selflessly may not be second nature, but preferring one another is always a choice we can make!*

Ron puts others before himself.

I can remember a time when the boys were small and our finances thin. It was back-to-school shoe-shopping time. My oldest son was admiring a sharp pair of sport shoes in the mirror when he caught sight of his dad behind him. "When are you getting new shoes, Daddy? Yours don't look so good!"

He was right. They were pretty raggedy. "Tonight, Cam, it's about getting you guys ready for school. I'll get mine later," Ron replied.

It was a long time ago, but I can still recall feeling my heart swell, reminding me how blessed I am to be Ron's wife. Better than any bunch of roses or fancy dinner out, this was real life. Our life.

Living sacrificially and selflessly comes with great challenges. I was raised as an only child, even though I wasn't. My only sibling, my brother Jack, was sixteen years older than me. When I was three he went away to college, and he moved even farther away after graduation, so I was an "only" for all practical purposes.

It was a good gig, actually. No need to share my toys. No "give half to your brother" requirements. I had my parents' undivided attention, and as the long-awaited baby girl, most of that attention was good.

What I missed, however, was the gift that comes when raised with brothers and sisters. Learning that if there's just one cookie left, perhaps you should give it to your sister, or at the very least, split it. Living with hand-me-downs. Christmas mornings with fewer toys and a stocking full of tangerines and apples. That was not my life. I missed some important lessons.

Ron's been a great example and has been patient with what you might call my slow growth in learning to prefer others. I *can* do it, and when I do, it's an unexpected joy. But it's still usually a conscious choice for me—it's work—it doesn't come without specific intent.

Jesus is always going to be first in our lives, and it's his example of sacrificial living that serves as our pattern. What I've learned is when Ron puts me ahead of himself, and I return the favor, we are in great shape.

Seeing the preparation Ron made to help me slip quickly into bed that night had the same impact on me as our long-ago shoe-shopping excursion. I quickly undressed and snuggled into his warmth. He stirred just slightly, long enough to kiss the top of my head and tell me to get my cold feet back on my side of the bed. It made me smile. Grateful. Blessed. Preferred.

> *Conventional wisdom: "Selflessness is to be concerned more with the needs and wishes of others than with one's own; unselfish."*
>
> —MERRIAM-WEBSTER DICTIONARY

Chapter 31 Choice Questions:
I Choose to Prefer You

1. Putting *yourself* first has become popular in our society, advancing the idea that you can't take care of other's needs until you've taken care of your own. What's your reaction to that concept?

2. When it comes to preferring your spouse, does it come naturally for you, or do you find it difficult? How challenging will it be—and what will you need to do—to set aside your own preferences?

3. Start small. Suggest the restaurant you know your spouse loves but you don't care for. Go to the movie that wouldn't be your first choice but is at the top of his list. Rise early on a really cold morning to warm up the car for her. Starting today, what choices will you make to honor God by preferring the concerns, needs, or wishes of your spouse?

Use the prayer below to declare your choice—or create one of your own.

Prayer: Jesus, you are the greatest example of selflessness. You left the majesty of heaven and came to a world undeserving of such a gift. You suffered penalty for crimes you did not commit and went to the cross without a word of defense. "Me first!" was never your cry, even though you alone deserve that position. I ask you to help me lay aside my wants, needs, and preferences for those of others, specifically my spouse. There is joy in supplying, caring for, and considering others. I desire to honor your Word in doing so. Remind me, Holy Spirit, to choose—to prefer—the one I love when the moment comes.

RESOURCES

BANNER SCRIPTURES FOR MEMORY

GOD, *train me in your ways of wise living.*

I'll transfer to my lips all the counsel that comes from your mouth;

I delight far more in what you tell me about living than in gathering a pile of riches.

I ponder every morsel of wisdom from you, I attentively watch how you've done it.

I relish everything you've told me of life, I won't forget a word of it.

—PSALM 119:12-16 (THE MESSAGE)

1. I CHOOSE TO ACCEPT GOD'S WORD AS THE BLUEPRINT FOR OUR LIFE

Every scripture is inspired by God and is useful for teaching, for showing mistakes, for correcting, and for training character.

—2 TIMOTHY 3:16

2. I CHOOSE TO PURSUE YOU

As for husbands, love your wives just like Christ loved the church and gave himself for her.

—Ephesians 5:25

3. I CHOOSE TO LOVE YOU

Rushing waters can't quench love; rivers can't wash it away. If someone gave all his estate in exchange for love, he would be laughed to utter shame.

—Song of Songs 8:7

4. I CHOOSE TO BLESS YOU

Then he blessed the children and went away from there.

—Matthew 19:15

5. I CHOOSE TO HONOR YOU

Love each other like the members of your family. Be the best at showing honor to each other.

—Romans 12:10

6. I CHOOSE TO KEEP MY COMMITMENT TO YOU

When a man makes a solemn promise to the Lord or swears a solemn pledge of binding obligation for himself, he cannot break his word. He must do everything he said.

—Numbers 30:2

7. I CHOOSE TO BE LOYAL TO YOU

Many people will say that they are loyal, but who can find a reliable person?

—PROVERBS 20:6

8. I CHOOSE TO TRUST YOU

Love puts up with all things, trusts in all things, hopes for all things, endures all things.

—1 CORINTHIANS 13:7

9. I CHOOSE TO FORGIVE YOU

Be kind, compassionate, and forgiving to each other, in the same way God forgave you in Christ.

—EPHESIANS 4:32

10. I CHOOSE TO BE ADAPTABLE

There's a season for everything and a time for every matter under the heavens.

—ECCLESIASTES 3:1

11. I CHOOSE TO SUBMIT TO YOU

Always give thanks to God the Father for everything in the name of our Lord Jesus Christ; and submit to each other out of respect for Christ.

—EPHESIANS 5:20-21

12. I CHOOSE TO SHARE YOUR BURDENS

Carry each other's burdens, and in this way you will fulfill the law of Christ.

—GALATIANS 6:2 NIV

13. I CHOOSE TO SERVE YOU

But the one who is greatest among you will be your servant.

—MATTHEW 23:11

14. I CHOOSE TO BE GENEROUS WITH YOU

Tell them to do good, to be rich in the good things they do, to be generous, and to share with others.

—1 TIMOTHY 6:18

15. I CHOOSE INTIMACY WITH YOU

I belong to my lover and my lover belongs to me.

—SONG OF SONGS 6:3

16. I CHOOSE TO KEEP ROMANCE ALIVE

Kiss me and kiss me again, for your love is sweeter than wine.

—SONG OF SONGS 1:2 (NLT)

17. I CHOOSE TO STAND IN AGREEMENT WITH YOU

Can two walk together, unless they are agreed?

—AMOS 3:3 (NKJV)

18. I CHOOSE TO CHALLENGE YOU

As iron sharpens iron, so a friend sharpens a friend.

—PROVERBS 27:17 (NLT)

19. I CHOOSE TO BE OPEN AND HONEST WITH YOU

Instead, by speaking the truth with love, let's grow in every way into Christ.

—EPHESIANS 4:15

20. I CHOOSE TO LISTEN TO YOU

You hear with your ears, but you don't really listen.

—ISAIAH 42:20 (NLT)

21. I CHOOSE TO LAUGH WITH YOU

A joyful heart helps healing, but a broken spirit dries up the bones.

—PROVERBS 17:22

22. I CHOOSE TO ACKNOWLEDGE YOU

Thank you for making me so wonderfully complex! Your workmanship is marvelous—how well I know it.

—PSALM 139:14 (NLT)

23. I CHOOSE TO BELIEVE IN YOU

I'm sure about this: the one who started a good work in you will stay with you to complete the job by the day of Christ Jesus.

—Philippians 1:6

24. I CHOOSE TO HELP YOU ACHIEVE YOUR DREAMS AND GOALS

Hope deferred makes the heart sick, but a dream fulfilled is a tree of life.

—Proverbs 13:12 (NLT)

25. I CHOOSE TO CELEBRATE YOUR SUCCESS

Be happy with those who are happy, and cry with those who are crying.

—Romans 12:15

26. I CHOOSE TO INVEST IN YOU

Instead of each person watching out for their own good, watch out for what is better for others.

—Philippians 2:4

27. I CHOOSE TO COMFORT YOU

Therefore comfort each other and edify one another, just as you also are doing.

—1 Thessalonians 5:11 (NKJV)

28. I CHOOSE TO LIVE IN PEACE WITH YOU

If possible, to the best of your ability, live at peace with all people.

—ROMANS 12:18

29. I CHOOSE TO SUPPORT YOU

Two people are better off than one, for they can help each other succeed.

—ECCLESIASTES 4:9 (NLT)

30. I CHOOSE TO PRAY FOR YOU

The prayer of the righteous person is powerful in what it can achieve.

—JAMES 5:16

31. I CHOOSE TO PREFER YOU

Submit to each other out of respect for Christ.

—EPHESIANS 5:21

ADDITIONAL CONVENTIONAL WISDOM

God always gives his best to those who leave the choice with him. —*Jim Elliot*

Every choice you make has an end result. —*Zig Ziglar*

Of the blessings set before you, make your choice, and be content. —*Samuel Johnson*

No one else can ever make your choices for you. Your choices are yours alone. They are as much a part of you as every breath you will take, every moment of your life. —*Unknown*

Destiny is no matter of chance. It is a matter of choice. It is not a thing to be waited for, it is a thing to be achieved. —*William Jennings Bryan*

The choices we make in the heat of emotion would be better if left for some other day. —*Shad Helmstetter*

Be miserable. Or motivate yourself. Whatever has to be done, it's always your choice. —*Wayne Dyer*

The end result of your life here on earth will always be the sum total of the choices you made while you were here. —*Shad Helmstetter*

Choose something today that your future self will thank you for. —*Unknown*

It's the scary choices that end up being the most worthwhile. —*Melissa Joy Kong*

The real act of marriage takes place in the heart, not in the ballroom or church or synagogue. It's a choice you make—not just on your wedding day, but over and over again—and that choice is reflected in the way you treat your husband or wife. —*Barbara De Angelis*

Pessimist: One who, when he has the choice of two evils, chooses both. —*Oscar Wilde*

If you have to choose between being right or being kind, choose kindness. —*Unknown*

Everything in your life is a reflection of a choice you've made. If you want a different result, make a different choice. —*Unknown*

When you have to make a choice and don't make it, that is in itself a choice. —*William James*

We are not animals. We are not a product of what has happened to us in our past. We have the power of choice. —*Stephen Covey*

You've only got three choices in life: Give up. Give in. Or give it all you've got. —*Unknown*

We need to teach the next generation of children from day one that they are responsible for their lives. Mankind's greatest gift, also its greatest curse, is that we have free choice. We can make our choices built from love or from fear. —*Elisabeth Kubler-Ross*

Happiness is a choice that requires effort at times. —*Aeschylus*

It is only when you exercise your right to choose that you can also exercise your right to change. —*Unknown*

The remarkable thing is, we have a choice every day regarding the attitude we will embrace for that day. —*Chuck R. Swindoll*

There may be a thousand little choices in a day. All of them count. —*Shad Helmstetter*

As human beings we are endowed with freedom of choice, and we cannot shuffle off our responsibility upon the shoulders of God or nature. We must shoulder it ourselves. It is our responsibility. —*Arnold J. Toynbee*

Discipline is just choosing between what you want now, for what you want most. —*Unknown*

Love is a choice you make from moment to moment. —*Barbara De Angelis*

Choice is what enables us to tell the world who we are and what we care about. —*Barry Schwartz*

I am who I am today because of the choices I made yesterday. —*Eleanor Roosevelt*

No matter what the situation, always remind yourself: I have a choice. —*Unknown*

At any given moment, you have the power to say, "This is not how the story is going to end." —*Christine Mason Miller*

If you don't like where you are in life, change it. You are not a tree. —*Unknown*

You have brains in your head and feet in your shoes. You can steer yourself any direction you choose! —*Dr. Seuss*

Do what's right, not what's easy! —*Unknown*

Love is a choice you make every day. —*Gary Chapman*

Every time you feel like doing the wrong thing, but choose to do the right thing—you are growing. —*Joyce Meyer*

Choose progress over perfection. —*Unknown*

God always gives his best to those who leave the choice with him. —*Jim Elliott*

Choose your love, love your choice. —*Thomas S. Monson*

Choosing to be positive and having a grateful attitude is going to determine how you're going to live your life.
—*Joel Osteen*

It's choice, not chance, that determines your destiny.
—*Jean Nidetch*

ACKNOWLEDGMENTS

To Ron: It was so much fun reflecting back on our life together as I wrote this book. Thanks for choosing me. I choose you too—today and every day.

With gratitude to my family: We are a group of truly imperfect individuals who love each other fiercely, even when we disagree. I accept each of you as you are and pray you return the favor. We love God, we forgive quickly, and we hold one another as treasured, because God placed us in this bunch to do life together. Thanks for your love and support.

Thank you to Lil Copan, Julie Gwinn, Cat Hoort, Brenda Smotherman, Katie Johnston, Kris Bears, and the folks at Abingdon for their amazing support and their belief in this book.

A special nod to Kathy Carlton Willis; Greg Johnson; Alice Bair Crider; WordServe Literary; Cliff and Trisha Hare; Mona and Gary Shriver; Becky and Greg Johnson; Jane and Jim Blicharz; Jayne; Karen; Loree; Susan; my mother-in-law, Virginia Rolin; and my personal prayer warrior and best friend, Cindy Smith. Some are contributors, some are cheerleaders—and a girl can never have too many of either. My relationship with each of you is unique and I am indebted to you for choosing to care about my work and me. Thank you.

NOTES

Chapter 6: I Choose to Keep My Commitment to You

H. Wallace Goddard, "Commitment in Healthy Relationships," *The Forum* 12:1 (Spring 2007). http://ncsu.edu/ffci/publications/2007/ v12-n1-2007-spring/godddard/fa-10-goddard.php